D1627488

WALTHAM FOREST LIBRARIES

904 000 00442196

WU 五穀 GU

by blue eye dragon

by blue eye dragon

Jade and Muriel Chen

A mother's recipes through her daughter's eyes

NH
NEW HOLLAND

ACKNOWLEDGEMENTS

To my dad and my brother Chris, thank you for always being there supporting me.

To Melissa, what would Marcus, Xavier, Lucius and Odin do without you? Best Gu-Gu ever.

To Mummy (Sri), you are just amazing, you made everything sound so simple. I admire you.

To Dad (Harry), thank you for your support and patience.

To Michelle, you will always be the one and only Lao-Shi! Thank you for the guidance.

To Amanda, you are the sister I never had, thank you for having my back.

To Yuni, Sugi, Jimmy and Alicia, my extended family, thank you for all your love and hard work.

To Fiona, thank you for still believing in me and mum! You are unbelievably brave and crazy to give me another book.

Waltham Forest Libraries	
904 000 00442196	
Askews & Holts	17-Nov-2015
641.5951 WU	£16.99
4842929	C

DEDICATION

There are two people in this world would would carry the load of my shoulder any time, and with a smile! They have both spoiled me, believed in me, and loved me for who I am!

Mum, I am so grateful to be your daughter. I will never be able to say enough thank you for what you have done for me, David and the boys.

David, I am so lucky to have found you! My world changed the day I met you. We now have four gorgeous boys and a life that will continue to get stronger! I wish I had found you earlier!

Contents

Introduction

MUM'S COOKING – SIMPLE, UNCOMPLICATED AND WITH LOVE

'Colour, aroma and taste should be the most important elements of cooking' as mum always says. This is also an old saying in Chinese/Taiwanese culture.

My mum, Jade, has always been the cook, not just for us, but for everyone else as well. Whenever there is a family or friends gathering, mum would always be the person in charge of cooking.

Sometimes, we would arrived at grandma's house, and an apron would be handed over to her with ingredients already prepared and ready to be cooked.

Not once has mum ever complained, instead she always does it with a big smile on her face, whether it was back then at those gathering or now when cooking in our family restaurants, Blue Eye Dragon and Wu-Gu. This is what I call love! Mum loves cooking, she loves the process, and the end result!

Mum grew up in Yangmei in Taiwan. From the age of 13 mum learnt traditional Taiwanese cooking from my grandmother. While I was growing up mum and dad ran several successful restaurants in Taiwan, for around 25 years. The major influences in their cooking came from the Hakka and Hokkien regions in China where our ancestors were from. In their restaurants, mum and dad would serve traditional Taiwanese favourite, with a special touch of home style cooking. I've enjoyed every minute I helped out in their restaurants. I loved the interaction with customers, the rush and the fun. It was a challenge to get everything right every day.

Blue Eye Dragon opened in September 2005 on Harris Street in Pyrmont and in March 2010, it was relocated to where we are today at the St Bede's Church Hall on Pyrmont Street. Just when mum thought she could take a back step and relax with all her grandchildren, I opened up Wu-Gu in February 2015, which brought out some of the delicious traditional noodles and soups in mum, most of which feature in this book.

The food we serve at Blue Eye Dragon and Wu-Gu is the food we eat at home. A Taiwanese Journalist once asked mum about the menu, asking what her reasoning was for the menu she has lovingly put together. Her answer was simple, 'It's what Muriel likes to eat, and what she wants to eat'.

I believe I can only serve the food that I love. Serving food I love makes it effortless for me to present to the diners that come through the door. 'If the food is not good enough to be on our dinner table, we don't serve it to our customers,' Mum always says.

The recipes in this book are mum's life of work, and a compilation of my favourite foods to eat! I hope you all enjoy the reading and creating the dishes in this book for your loved ones, and that these dishes become as much a part of your family as they are ours.

TAIWANESE FOOD: A BALANCE OF FLAVOURS

Customers often ask why our food is different from most Chinese restaurants and the answer is 'we are from Taiwan and, most importantly, they are my Mum's recipes'.

Most Taiwanese people are from China and our food is heavily influenced by Chinese cooking.

In addition to China's influence, Taiwan also has some Japanese flavours, as Japan occupied Taiwan for half a century from 1895. You'll often find Japanese dishes in Taiwanese restaurants, especially seafood restaurants.

Taiwan is probably most famous for its roadside food stalls rather than banquet dining. This style of food is the result of a highly competitive market, with small food business operators constantly needing to invent new flavours and dishes in order to survive.

Taiwanese cuisine is a mixing pot of good food from all over China and its use of local produce and creativity sets it apart from other Asian food. Blending together food from different provinces makes Taiwanese food a balance of all the flavours.

BASICS

In today's modern, busy life we tend to work longer hours and have less time for everything else. If you follow the basics in this section, cooking a meal for four people in 30 minutes will be easy. After each grocery shopping trip, Mum always takes the time to clean, cut and marinate everything, and only then stores them in the fridge or freezer. This means she can cook a meal for six of us in a very short time.

Serving sizes

All the stir-fry dishes make one serve only. All the entrée dishes are small, but can be doubled for a main dish. If you are cooking for more than one serve, try not to double the quantities. Instead, either make a second amount separately or, even better, make a different dish and share! Mum always asks, 'How many people for dinner?', then she will always cook an extra dish. For example, for four people, she will always make five dishes.

Marinating should be very simple and easy, as you don't want to mask the natural flavours of the produce. One thing that's very important to us at blue eye dragon is the freshness and clean cut taste of the food.

Storing the meat or seafood in serving quantity portions of around 250 g (8 oz) makes preparation quicker and less messy. For quick defrosting, pack each portion flat.

Chicken and Pork

Whether it is chicken thigh or breast fillet, it is important to trim away the fat before cooking because this makes a difference to the taste. With chicken, unlike beef or pork, you need to cut along the grain.

Pork is a beautiful *pink* meat that Asians love! Pork cheek is the best for stir-frying texturewise, but it's hard to get. If you are concerned about fat, lean pork or pork loin are good. Pork is tougher than chicken so thinly slice against the grain.

To marinate 1 kg (2 lb) of chicken or pork:
½ teaspoon salt
1 teaspoon sugar
2 tablespoons potato flour (see Glossary)
60 ml (2 fl oz) water
2 tablespoons vegetable oil

Mix all the ingredients except the oil together using a lifting motion with your hands, until you can feel the water has been absorbed by the meat.
Add the vegetable oil and mix well.
Freeze in airtight containers in desired serving portions.

Beef

Beef skirt steak or flank steak is best for stir-frying. It is more expensive than the normal lean beef, but it is definitely worth the money. Make sure you cut against the grain, otherwise it will end up as chewy as beef jerky!

To marinate 1 kg (2 lb) of beef:
1 teaspoon sugar
½ egg, beaten
2 tablespoons potato flour (see Glossary)
1 tablespoon soy sauce
120 ml (4 fl oz) water
2 tablespoons vegetable oil

Note: do not use salt if marinating beef

Mix all the ingredients except the oil together using a lifting motion with your hands, until you can feel the water has been absorbed by the meat.
Add the vegetable oil and mix well.
Freeze in airtight containers in desired serving portions.

Prawns and Fish

To preserve freshness, peel and devein the prawns before marinating.

When freezing fresh (not peeled or marinated) prawns, it is best to freeze them in water.

To marinate 1 kg (2 lb) of prawns:
¼ teaspoon salt
½ teaspoon sugar
3 tablespoons cornflour
ground white pepper, a pinch
1 egg white

Mix all the ingredients together and add to prawns. Freeze in airtight containers in desired serving portions.

Fish fillets should be cleaned and frozen in desired serving portions. If freezing a whole fish, make sure the fish is cleaned and gutted thoroughly. Then freeze in an airtight container.

Storing vegetables

There is an old Chinese saying: 'Money knows quality'. This means that expensive produce is expensive for a reason: it's the best. Of course, the best vegetables are always those in season. Vegetables are the hardest of the stir-fry ingredients to keep fresh, so mum always purchases the best and spends time washing them and removing any yellow or loose leaves prior to storing them in airtight containers. This means we have coriander (cilantro) and basil in the restaurant that tastes as fresh as if they were just picked from the garden.

Mum frequently jokes that she treats the vegetables as well as she treats us; with lots of love and care.

Deep-frying

At blue eye dragon we do all our deep-frying in a deep fryer so we can set the temperature just by using the dial. If you don't have a deep fryer then heat the oil in a wok. To test if it is at 180°C (350°F), the normal temperature for deep-frying, place a small cube of bread into the hot oil. If it browns within 1 minute it's hot enough.

Stir-frying in a wok

The main things to remember when stir-frying are to always to heat up the wok before adding the oil, and then make sure that it's very hot before beginning to stir-fry. Also you must never stir-fry large amounts, otherwise the results will be stewed. If you wish to make a larger portion try to make the dish twice, don't just double the quantities in one wok.

> ### Note
> To save freezer space, use cling film for each portion then place several packets in one airtight container.

Sauces

XO Sauce

Caramelised
Kong-Bao
Sauce

Dumpling
Sauce for
Dumplings

Taiwanese
Garlic Five
Spice Sauce

Garlic Chilli Sauce
with Chilli Beans

Fish Sauce

Sauces

Stir-frying is about balancing the beautiful flavours of all the ingredients—add too much sauce and the dish becomes stewed! Salt and sugar are normally enough for a light flavoured dish as the ingredients, blended together in a very hot wok, will become surprisingly tasty.

In Taiwan, most stir-frying does not involve lots of sauces; the most frequent and popular sauce Taiwanese cooking uses is soy sauce and its quality determines how good a dish tastes.

Here are some ready-made bottled sauces that can be purchased in Asian grocery stores. They are a must for the pantry and are what we use at our restaurants.

Kim Ve Wong Soy Sauce
Kim Lam Soy Paste
Kong Yang Black Vinegar
Kong Yang Rice Vinegar

In addition to these sauces, here is a list of the essential herbs and spices used throughout this book to make stir-fried food easy to make and tasty too.

Five spice powder
Ground white pepper
Garlic
Shallots (spring onions/scallions)
Ginger
Chilli
Coriander (cilantro)
Star anise

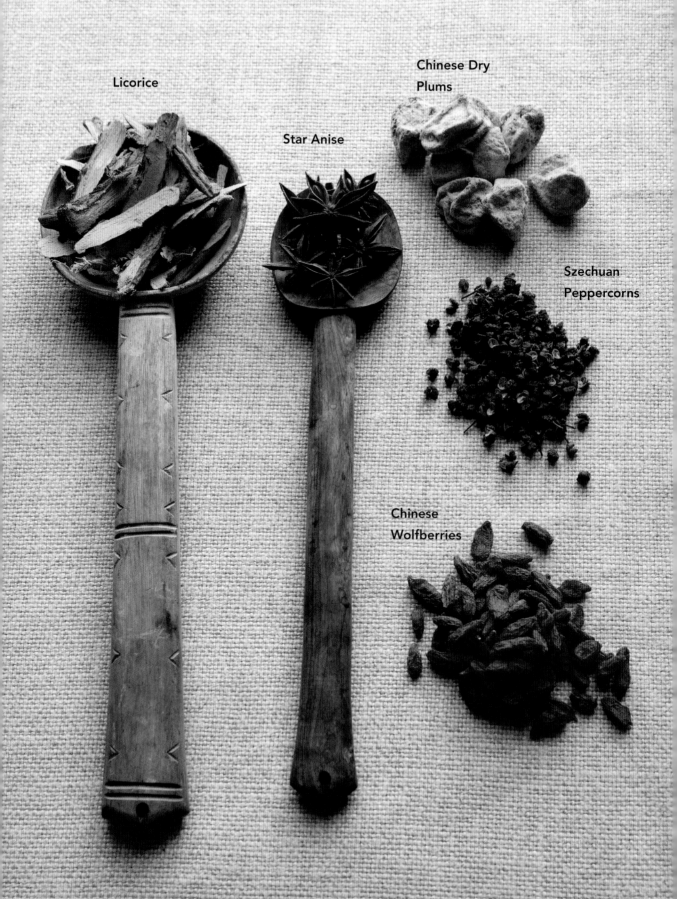

Licorice

Star Anise

Chinese Dry Plums

Szechuan Peppercorns

Chinese Wolfberries

Taiwanese Sweet and Sour Sauce

2½ tablespoons sugar
¼ tablespoon black vinegar (see Glossary)
½ teaspoon soy sauce
125 ml (4 fl oz) water
1 teaspoon potato flour (see Glossary)

Combine potato flour with 1 teaspoon of water to make a paste. Mix all the ingredients in a big pot, bring to the boil and stir in the paste to thicken the sauce.

Allow to cool before storing in bottles to refrigerate.

Makes 1 cup

Sweet and Sour Sauce

250 ml (8 fl oz) water
250 ml (8 fl oz) tomato sauce
250 ml (8 fl oz) sugar
250 ml (8 fl oz) rice vinegar (see Glossary)
¼ teaspoon preserved Chinese plum powder (optional—see Glossary)

Combine all ingredients and bring to the boil. Allow to cool before storing in bottles to refrigerate.

Makes 4 cups

Caramelised Kong-Bao Sauce

Part One
125 ml (4 fl oz) sugar
125 ml (4 fl oz) water

Part Two
1 teaspoon ground white pepper
125 ml (4 fl oz) sugar
2 pieces white rock sugar (see Glossary)
100 ml (3.5 fl oz) soy sauce
125 ml (4 fl oz) black vinegar (see Glossary)
1 tablespoon glutinous rice flour (see Glossary)

Part One

Cook the sugar with half of the water in a wok, stirring continously. The mixture will turn red in colour then dark brown.

Add the rest of the water and stir well.

Part Two

Add all Part Two ingredients to part one and bring to the boil.

Combine the glutinous rice flour with 1 tablespoon of water to make a paste.

Add the paste to the wok and stir well until sauce thickens.

Allow to cool before storing in bottles to refrigerate.

Makes 2 cups

Fish Sauce

500 ml (16 fl oz) water
125 ml (4 fl oz) fish sauce
80g (2¾oz) white rock sugar (see Glossary)
3 slices dry licorice

In a pot, bring the water and dry licorice to the boil. Add all ingredients, stir and bring back to the boil. Remove the dry licorice. Allow to cool before storing in bottles to refrigerate.

This fish sauce is a milder taste and the licorice takes the flavour to another level.

Makes 3 cups

Jade's Bloody Plum Sauce

¼ tablespoon preserved Chinese plum powder (see Glossary)
125 ml (4 fl oz) rice vinegar (see Glossary)
½ black vinegar (see Glossary)
½ tablespoon Worcestershire sauce
250 ml (8 fl oz) tomato sauce
½ tablespoon HP sauce (steak sauce)
500 ml (16 fl oz) sugar
chilli oil, a drizzle (see Glossary)
250 ml (8 fl oz) water

In a pot, bring water and all ingredients to the boil. Stir constantly.
Allow to cool before storing in bottles to refrigerate.

Makes about 4 cups

Garlic Chilli Sauce with Chilli Beans

500 g (1 lb) small hot chillies, finely chopped
300 g (9½ oz) garlic, minced
1 litre (32 fl oz) vegetable oil
60 ml (2 fl oz) sesame oil
150g (5oz) chilli bean sauce (see Glossary)

Spread the chillies evenly over a large baking tray then sprinkle the garlic over the chillies.

Heat oil to 200°C (400°F) in a wok until almost smoking, then turn off the heat.

Use a large ladle to drizzle the hot oil all over the chillies and garlic, until all the garlic turns golden brown. Then stir the chillies and garlic together and continue to pour the hot oil over them.

Add the chilli beans sauce and sesame oil, then mix thoroughly. Allow to cool before storing in bottles to refrigerate.

Makes 6 cups

Note
To store the sauce in the fridge, make sure the chillies are fully covered in oil. If for any reason the oil is consumed faster than the chillies, add more sesame oil to cover.

Seafood Sauce (Hoi Sin Sauce)

2 tablespoons soy sauce
250 ml (8 fl oz) oyster sauce
80 ml (2¾ fl oz) rice wine
100 ml (3 fl oz) sugar

Mix all ingredients together on low heat. Stir through until sugar dissolves. Allow to cool before storing in bottles to refrigerate.

Makes 2 cups

Salt and
Pepper

Bai-Chao
(Hundred Spices)

Curry Powder

Cinnamon

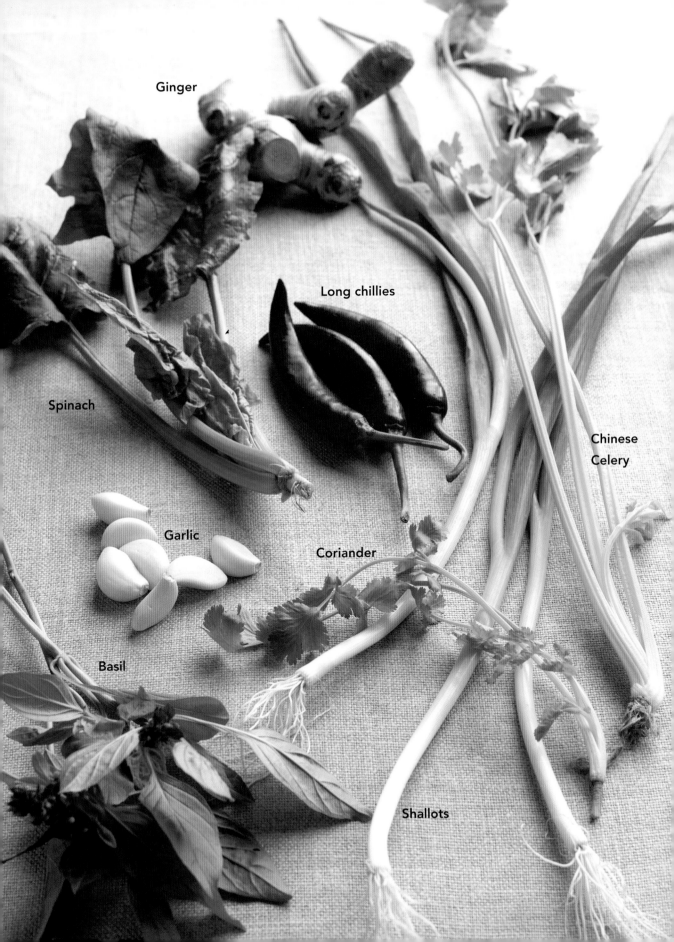

Ginger

Long chillies

Spinach

Chinese
Celery

Garlic

Coriander

Basil

Shallots

Dipping Sauce for Dumplings

25 ml (¾ fl oz) chilli paste
75 ml (2½ fl oz) soy sauce
1 teaspoon sesame oil
1 tablespoon rice vinegar

Mix all the ingredients. Store unused sauce in bottles to refrigerate.

Makes enough for several servings

Taiwanese Garlic Five Spice Sauce

This is great over squid, oysters and other seafood or as a barbecue marinade.

250 ml (8 fl oz) tomato sauce
60 ml (2 fl oz) sugar
60 ml (2 fl oz) soy paste (see Glossary)
60 ml (2 fl oz) black vinegar (see Glossary)
1 teaspoon sesame oil
1 teaspoon chilli oil (see Glossary)
2 shallots (spring onions/scallions), finely chopped
10 slices ginger, finely chopped
5 cloves garlic, finely chopped
1 large red chilli, finely chopped or deseeded if required
1 small bunch coriander (cilantro), finely chopped

Combine tomato sauce, sugar, soy paste, vinegar, sesame oil and chilli oil, then stir until sugar has dissolved.

Add the shallots, ginger, garlic, chilli and coriander and mix well.

Makes 2 cups

Note
This makes a large quantity and unused sauce can be refrigerated in airtight bottles.

Entrées,
Side Dishes and
Condiments

Deep-Fried Crumbed Chicken Fillets

250 g (8 oz) chicken breast fillets
2 teaspoons salt and pepper mixture (see Salt and Pepper section)
½ teaspoon curry powder
2 eggs, lightly beaten
vegetable oil
500 g (16 oz) cornflour
500 g (16 oz) breadcrumbs

Trim each fillet into palm-sized pieces, making sure they are all the same thickness to ensure even cooking.

Combine a pinch of the salt and pepper mixture, curry powder and ½ tablespoon of the lightly beaten egg. Marinate the chicken and allow to rest for about 5 minutes.

Heat the oil in a deep fryer (or wok, see Basics) to 180°C (350°F).

On both sides, lightly dust the chicken fillets with the cornflour and then coat with the remaining beaten egg, before covering evenly with breadcrumbs.

Allow to stand for about a minute before deep-frying.

Once the chicken starts to float and turn golden brown they are cooked. Drain them on paper towels to absorb excess oil.

Cut the chicken fillets into long strips and serve with the remaining salt and pepper mixture on the side.

One serve

> Note
> Left over trimmed chicken pieces can be kept
> to make huntuns (wontons).

Crispy Chicken Wings

Marinade
2 cloves garlic, minced
1 teaspoon salt
1 teaspoon sugar
1 teaspoon curry powder
½ egg, lightly beaten
ground white pepper, a pinch
2 tablespoons cornflour

1 kg (2 lb) chicken wings (about 12 wings, mid section only)
500 g (1 lb) sweet potato flour (preferably crumbed—see Glossary)
1 tablespoon salt and pepper mixture (see Salt and Pepper section)
vegetable oil, for deep-frying

Combine the marinade ingredients and rub onto the chicken wings.

Heat the oil in a deep fryer (or wok, see Basics) to 180°C (350°F).

Coat the wings with the sweet potato flour, making sure they are well covered.

Allow to rest for about 1 minute.

Shake off any excess flour and place the wings in the deep fryer.

Once the chicken starts to float and turn golden brown they are cooked. Drain them on paper towels to absorb excess oil.

Sprinkle some of the salt and pepper mixture evenly over the chicken. Serve with the remaining salt and pepper mixture on the side.

One serve

Crispy Chicken with Basil and Five Spice

3 teaspoons salt and pepper mixture (see Salt and Pepper section)
½ teaspoon five spice powder (see Glossary)
salt, a pinch
sugar, a pinch
250 g (8 oz) chicken fillet, cut into 2 x 1 cm (¾x½ in) pieces
250 g (8 oz) cornflour or sweet potato flour (see Glossary)
125 g (4 oz) basil leaves

Combine the salt and pepper mixture and the five spice powder in a spice grinder or mortar until well blended. Set aside.

Marinate the chicken in a pinch of cornflour, salt and sugar and stand for a few minutes.

Heat the oil in a deep fryer (or wok, see Basics) to 180°C (350°F).

Lightly dust the chicken pieces with the remaining cornflour, then let them rest for about a minute before deep-frying.

Once the chicken pieces start to float and turn golden brown they are cooked. Drain them on paper towels to absorb excess oil.

Before putting the basil in the deep fryer, make sure you have the lid handy, as the basil will cause the oil to splatter. Fry the basil for 1 minute until crisp. Drain the basil.

In a big bowl, toss the chicken pieces with the basil and sprinkle with some of the salt and pepper and five spice mixture.

To serve, place the chicken on a plate, top with the basil and place remaining salt and pepper and five spice mixture on the side.

One serve

> Note
> Sweet potato flour gives a much crispier texture.

Chicken Roll with Water Chestnuts and Hundred Spices

200 g (6.5 oz) chicken fillet, cut into long strips
1 teaspoon ground white pepper
2 tablespoons potato flour (see Glossary)
250 g (8 oz) onion, diced
200 ml (7 fl oz) water chestnuts (canned), diced
1 teaspoon Bai-Chao (Hundred Spices—see Glossary)
½ teaspoon five spice powder (see Glossary)

4 pieces bean curd pastry, 20 cm (8 in) square (see Glossary)
1 teaspoon plain flour
Vegetable oil, for frying

Dipping Sauce
1 tablespoon chilli paste
1 tablespoon sweet chilli sauce

coriander (cilantro), to serve

Mix all the dry ingredients together with the onion.

Open up the bean curd pastry with the corner pointed towards you. Spread the onion mixture evenly to the centre of pastry, and then place chicken strips on top.

Combine the plain flour and 1 teaspoon of water to make a paste.

Roll up the pastry and seal the edges with the flour paste.

Heat the oil in a deep fryer (or wok, see Basics) to 180°C (350°F).

Fry the chicken roll until it floats then drain on paper towels to absorb excess oil.

Combine the chilli paste and sweet chilli sauce to make the dipping sauce.

Slice the roll with a sharp knife at an angle and serve with coriander and the dipping sauce.

One serve. Makes 4 rolls.

> Note
> Coriander is an absolute must for this dish as it really enhances the taste.

Chilli Chicken Huntuns (Wontons)

Filling
250 g (8 oz) minced chicken
salt, ground white pepper, sugar, a pinch
2 teaspoons potato flour (see Glossary)
1 tablespoon water

Sauces
1 teaspoon Garlic Chilli Sauce with Chilli Beans (see Sauces)
2 tablespoons Dumpling Sauce for Dumplings (see Sauces)

coriander (cilantro), to serve
1 packet huntun (wonton) pastry (see Glossary)
¼ lettuce, shredded, to serve

Mix together the filling ingredients until the water is absorbed into the chicken.

Place one teaspoon of chicken mince in the centre of a huntun pastry. Spread the mixture out over two-thirds of the pastry. Spreading out the filling means a pocket of air is left inside the pastry which makes them float.

Gather the edges of the pastry at the top. Pinch and twist to seal the top lightly. Repeat with the rest of the pastry and mince.

Bring a large pot of water to the boil. Place the huntuns in the boiling water, stirring occasionally to avoid them from sticking to the pot. Once they float to the surface, wait a further two minutes, then drain them and put into a mixing bowl.

Stir in the sauces then serve the huntuns on top of the shredded lettuce. Garnish with coriander to serve.

Two serves

> ### Note
> Huntun can be premade and frozen in airtight containers. Freeze them individually to shape before packing in a container.

Tea-Smoked Chicken

1 kg (2 lb) chicken drumsticks
2 litres (3 ½ pints) water
60 g (2 oz) ginger, sliced
2 shallots (spring onions/scallions)
½ tablespoon sugar
125 ml (4 fl oz) tea
1 tablespoon salt

Bring the water to the boil in a big pot. Add ginger, shallots, salt and chicken drumsticks. Bring back to the boil, then simmer for 15 minutes. Remove and drain wings.

Line a wok with foil. Spread the tea and sugar across the foil and place the drumsticks on a mesh stand in the wok.

Place the wok over medium heat and cover with a lid to steam the chicken. When you can see 'yellow' smoke, turn off the heat and let it rest for 2–3 minutes, before you open the lid. The colour should be light brown. When the wings cool down the colour will darken.

One serve

Note
Traditionally in Taiwan we smoke the whole chicken. This recipe can be used with any part of the chicken or the whole chicken, with the skin on.

Fried Shallots

Fried Shallots are commonly used in an array of Asian dishes. South East Asian countries use them on salads, fried rice and soup and in Taiwan, it is a must for noodle soups. To enhance the flavour of the shallots, they can be fried in pork fat.

2 kg (4 lb) red shallots, skinned and thinly sliced

500 ml (16fl oz) vegetable oil

Heat up the wok and add the oil on high heat. Once hot, add in the shredded shallots, 1 handful at a time while stirring continuously. Once the moisture has vaporised, moved the wok to medium heat.

It is very important to continuously stir the shallots during the frying process to prevent the shallots from sticking and burning as a result of caramelisation.

Once the shallots begin to brown, quickly drain them and spread them evenly on a tray to cool. The shallots will continue browning from the heat after they have been removed from the wok.

Repeat the process until all shallots have been fried. The oil can be reused until all shallots are done. If required, add more oil for easier frying.

Prawn Spring Rolls

Filling

160 g (5 oz) water chestnuts (canned), diced

100 g (4 oz) yellow chives, cut into 2 cm (¾ in) pieces (see Glossary)

30 g (1 oz) shallots (spring onions/scallions), finely chopped

¼ teaspoon salt

¼ teaspoon sugar

1 tablespoon potato flour (see Glossary)

½ tablespoons bonito powder (see Glossary)

600 g (1¼ lb) prawns (shrimp), peeled, deveined and diced

1 tablespoon plain flour

30 sheets spring roll pastry (10 cm/4 in size) (see Glossary)

1 piece nori paper, cut into cm (¼ in) x 10 cm (4 in) strips

vegetable oil – for frying

coriander (cilantro), to serve

2 tablespoons Plum Sauce (see Sauces)

Combine all the filling ingredients except for the yellow chives and shallots. Then add the yellow chives and shallots and mix well.

Mix the plain flour with 1 tablespoon of water to make a paste.

Fill a spring roll pastry with a tablespoon of the mixture. Spread the mixture evenly over half of the pastry. Roll it up and seal with the flour paste.

Wrap a strip of nori around the centre of each roll, secure with flour paste.

Repeat with the remaining pastry and filling.

Heat up enough oil to deep-fry the rolls in a deep fryer (or wok, see Basics) to 180°C (350°F).

Fry the rolls until they start to float and are lightly brown. Drain on paper towels to remove excess oil.

Serve with some coriander and plum sauce on the side.

Makes 30

Spicy Chicken Wings
Caramelised in Soy Sauce

1 kg (2.2 lb) chicken wings (10–12 wings), mid-section
5 garlic cloves, crushed, skin on
1 small red chilli, chopped (or left out if serving for children)
1 shallot (spring onions/scallions), cleaned, whole
½ teaspoons sugar
60 ml (2 fl oz) soy sauce
125 ml (4 fl oz) water

To serve
sesame oil, to drizzle
cucumber slices, to garnish

Add all the ingredients in a wok and bring to the boil.

Simmer for 15 minutes and stir constantly. When cooked, turn on high heat to reduce the sauce and to caramelise. Drizzle with sesame oil and serve with cucumber slices.

One serve

Note
This dish tastes just as good when it is cool.
You can also barbecue the cooked wings for a different taste, great for picnics in the summer.

Note
Fresh dumplings need to be left in the freezer on a tray, to shape and harden
before being sealed in a container to store. Dumplings can be kept in the freezer
for up to 2 months and take 2 minutes more than fresh dumplings to cook.

Pork Dumplings

Filling
½ teaspoon salt
¾ teaspoon sugar
¾ teaspoon ground white pepper
1½ teaspoons ginger, minced
½ teaspoon soy sauce
80 ml (2.5 fl oz) water
500 g (1 lb) minced (ground) pork
150 g (5 oz) garlic chives, finely chopped

1 shallot (spring onions/scallions), green section only, finely chopped
2½ tablespoons potato flour (see Glossary)
sesame oil, a drizzle
dumpling pastry, 30–40 pieces (see Glossary)
Dipping Sauce for Dumplings (see Sauces)

Mix together all the filling ingredients until dissolved.

Add the mixture to the pork, using your hands to gradually mix together with a lifting motion until the water is absorbed.

In a separate bowl, mix the chives, shallots and potato flour together. Add this to the pork mixture and mix well. Finally, add the sesame oil and mix again.

Place 1 tablespoon of the pork filling in the centre of a piece of pastry. Dab around the edges with water. Fold the pastry together by pressing on the top edge of the pastry first, and then pleat the sides together to shape the dumpling.

Boil a large pot of water. Put the dumplings in the boiling water, stirring occasionally to avoid them from sticking. Turn down the heat once the water comes back to the boil. Dumplings should start to float after 4 minutes. Wait for another 2 minutes before removing them from the pot.

Serve with dipping sauce.

Alternatively, to pan-fry dumplings, place cooked dumplings on an oiled hot plate and fry until the bases of the dumplings are golden and crispy.

Makes 30–40 dumplings depending on filling sizes

Prawn Dumplings

Filling
500 g (1 lbs) prawns (shrimp), peeled, deveined and diced
25 g (1 oz) Chinese celery, chopped finely (see Glossary)
75 g (2½ oz) shallots (spring onions/scallions), chopped finely
150 g (9 oz) water chestnuts (canned), diced
½ teaspoon ground white pepper

25 g (1 oz) potato flour (see Glossary)
1 bag of dumpling pastry (see Glossary)
Dipping Sauce for Dumplings (see Sauces)

Mix together all the filling ingredients and then stir through the potato flour.

Place 1 tablespoon of the filling in the centre of a piece of pastry. Dab around the edges with water. Fold the pastry together by pressing on the top edge of the pastry first, and then pleat the sides together to shape the dumpling.

Boil a large pot of water. Put the dumplings in the boiling water, stirring occasionally to avoid them sticking. Turn down the heat once the water comes back to the boil. Dumplings should start to float after 6 minutes. Wait for another 2 minutes before removing them from the pot.

Serve with dipping sauce.

Alternatively, to pan fry dumplings, place cooked dumplings on an oiled hot plate and fry until the bases of the dumplings are golden and crispy.

Makes about 30 dumplings depending on filling size

Note
Fresh dumplings need to be left in the freezer on a tray, to shape and harden before being sealed in a container to store. Dumplings can be kept in the freezer for up to 2 months and take 2 minutes more than fresh dumplings to cook.

Stewed Beef Shin

2 kg (4 lb) beef shin (heel muscle)
1 tablespoon sesame oil to stir-fry

Spices
60 g (2 oz) ginger slices
10 whole cloves garlic, skin on
8 pieces star anise
1 teaspoon Szechuan peppercorns

Stewing Sauces
375 ml (12.5 fl oz) soy sauce
1.5 litre (48 fl oz) water
1 tablespoon rice wine
2 tablespoons chilli bean sauce (see Glossary)
1 tablespoon sugar
1 shallot (spring onion/scallion)

To serve
1 shallot (spring onion/scallion)
sesame oil, a drizzle
stewed sauces, a drizzle

> **Note**
> The remaining uncut beef shin can be stored in the freezer in airtight containers. Thaw in the fridge overnight before preparing to serve. The sauces can also be frozen.

Wash the beef shin then bring a big pot of water to the boil. Put in the beef shin and cook for about 5 minutes. Drain.

Heat up the wok and stir-fry the spices with sesame oil until fragrant.

In a pot, put stewing sauces, beef and the stir-fried spices together. Bring to the boil and simmer for about 1½ hours over low heat with the lid on.

Remove beef from the pot and allow to cool to room temperature, then thinly slice.

Garnish with shallots and drizzle with some of the stewed sauces and sesame oil when serving.

One serve

Boiled Pork Belly
with Basil and Chilli Sauce

Dipping Sauce
5 basil leaves, finely chopped
1 chilli, finely chopped
2 tablespoons soy sauce

250 g (8 oz) pork belly
60 g (2 oz) ginger, finely shredded, to serve

Combine all ingredients for the dipping sauce.

Wash pork belly and clean the skin with a knife. Mum always says she's giving the pork a good shave!

Bring water to the boil in a wok, put in the pork belly and simmer for 20–30 minutes

Take out the pork belly, let it cool down to warm before thinly slicing.

Wash shredded ginger well in water to reduce the sharpness of the ginger taste.

Serve the sliced pork belly with the shredded ginger and dipping sauce.

One serve

Note
This is a beautiful dish—easy
to make yet full of flavour.

Drunken Chicken

1 tablespoon Chinese wolfberries (see Glossary)
4 chicken breast fillets
50 g (2 oz) ginger, thinly sliced
2 tablespoons salt
2 tablespoons sugar
2 shallots (spring onions/scallions), chopped

Marinade
375 ml (12.5 fl oz) Shaoxing rice wine (see Glossary)
½ tablespoon salt
coriander (cilantro), to serve

Soften the wolfberries in water then dry on paper towels.

Bring some water to the boil in a pot, blanch the chicken quickly then remove from the water and drain.

Boil 1 litre (34 fl oz) of water, then add in the ginger, salt, sugar, shallots and chicken fillets. Cover and cook for 12 minutes over low heat. Remove the chicken and keep the stock.

Combine 350 ml (12 fl oz) of chicken stock with the wine and salt.

Allow to cool before adding in the chicken and wolfberries.

Refrigerate for 24 hours.

Slice the chicken fillets to 1 cm (½ in) thickness and serve with some wolfberries and coriander. The remaining chicken stock can be used for soups.

One serve

> Note
> Breast fillet can be replaced with thigh fillet if preferred.
> If the fillet has the skin on, it will give a much better texture.

Deep-Fried Prawns with Plum Sauce

salt and pepper mixture, a pinch (see Salt and Pepper section)
250 g (8 oz) cornflour
10 tiger prawns (shrimp), peeled, deveined, tail left on
vegetable oil
Plum Sauce (see Sauces)

Mix together the salt and pepper mixture and 1 tablespoon of cornflour.

Combine with the prawns and leave to marinate.

Heat the oil in a deep fryer (or wok, see Basics) to 180°C (350°F).

Coat the prawns with the remaining cornflour in a tray. Let the prawns set for about a minute before deep-frying. Prawns are cooked when curled and floating.

Remove the prawns. Drain on paper towels to absorb excess oil before serving on a plate with the plum sauce.

One serve

Note
If plum sauce is not available,
use sweet chilli sauce or salt
and pepper mixture.

Oysters with Spicy Taiwanese Garlic Sauce

12 oysters
125 ml (4 fl oz) Taiwanese Garlic Five Spice Sauce (see Sauces)
1 litre (1¾ pints) water

Bring water to the boil in a pot and quickly blanch the oysters.

Remove from the water, drain and put a teaspoon of the Taiwanese Garlic Five Spice Sauce over each one and serve.

One serve

Scallops with Shallots
and Fish Sauce

60 ml (2 fl oz) Fish Sauce (see Sauces)
12 scallops, cleaned, roe on or off depending on your preference
1 shallot (spring onion/scallion), finely julienned
2 slices of carrot, finely julienned

Mix shallots and carrots together.

Heat up the fish sauce and keep warm.

Bring some water to the boil in a pot. Place the scallops gently in the water and cook for about 1 minute, until their colour changes to white. Quickly remove them from the pot and onto a serving plate.

Top scallops with shallots and carrots, then spoon the fish sauce over each one.

One serve

Silken Tofu with Garlic Chives and Bonito Flakes

This is great to have with a glass of beer.

150 g (5 oz) 1 bunch garlic chives
1 packet of silken tofu
250 g (8 oz) bonito flakes (see Glossary)
soy paste, to drizzle (see Glossary)

Clean the chives well. Use cooking string to tie the chives together in a bunch.

Bring a pan of water to the boil and put the chives in for a few seconds. Remove immediately.

Cool the chives in the fridge.

Open the packet of tofu and tip them onto a serving plate. Cut to bite-sized pieces.

Just before serving, cut the chives into 5 cm (2 in) pieces and place them next to or on top of the tofu.

Sprinkle the bonito flakes over the chives, tofu and the plate, then drizzle with soy paste over the top.

One serve

> Note
> This is a beautiful summer dish. Fast, simple and full of flavour.

Vegetarian Spring Rolls

400 g (13 oz) cabbage, shredded
125 g (4 oz) carrots, shredded
250 g (8 oz) celery, shredded
2 tablespoons vegetable oil
½ teaspoon salt
½ teaspoon sugar
¼ teaspoon ground white pepper
3 tablespoons potato flour (see Glossary)
1 tablespoon plain flour
coriander (cilantro), to serve

Place the cabbage, carrots and celery in boiling water with the oil. Once the water comes back to the boil, drain vegetables very well.

In a big bowl, mix salt, sugar and pepper with the vegetables, then gradually add in the potato flour and mix well.

Mix the plain flour with 1 tablespoon of water to make a paste and set aside.

Fill a spring roll pastry with 2 tablespoons of the mixture. Spread the mixture evenly over half of the pastry. Roll it up and seal with the flour paste.

Repeat with the remaining pastry and filling.

Heat the oil in a deep fryer (or wok, see Basics) to 180°C (350°F).

Fry the rolls until they start to float and are lightly brown. Drain on paper towels to remove excess oil.

Serve with some coriander on the side.

Makes 20

Note
Don't roll the spring rolls too tightly or they will burst while deep-frying. You can freeze the spring rolls in an airtight container just before frying. For a faster deep-fry, microwave each roll for about 15 seconds.

Marinated Broccoli Stems

3 large broccoli stems, peeled and washed

Marinade
1 tablespoon salt
1 teaspoon sugar
3 cloves of garlic, sliced
1 small red chilli, deseeded and chopped
sesame oil, a drizzle

Cut broccoli into little finger-sized strips.

Marinate in salt only, until the stems are soft but still crunchy.

Wash salt off, combine remaining marinade ingredients with the broccoli and leave in the fridge until chilled.

Serve.

One serve

Note
You can add thinly sliced raw carrots for colour if you like. To my Mum, broccoli stems are like candy. She smiles when there are plenty for her to marinate. I love this dish and when I was a child, I frequently ate all of them before they made it to our dinner table.

Asparagus with Bonito Flakes and Soy Paste

This is a great summer dish. Serve warm or cold, as preferred.

1 teaspoon salt
250 g (8 oz) 1 bunch asparagus
250 g (8 oz) bonito flakes (see Glossary)
soy paste, to drizzle (see Glossary)

Bring a pan of water to the boil, add the salt and then put the asparagus in for about a minute.

Remove the asparagus from the water, cut into 5 cm (2 in) pieces and place on a serving plate.

Sprinkle asparagus with bonito flakes and then drizzle with the soy paste.

One serve

Note
When buying asparagus avoid those with white ends. This means they are old. Peel the skin with a peeler to reduce the white ends.

Lettuce Wraps

60 g (2 oz) pine nuts
125 g (4 oz) celery, chopped
125 g (4 oz) water chestnuts, chopped
125 g (4 oz) bamboo shoots, chopped
1 tablespoon carrot, chopped
8 large tiger prawns (shrimp), peeled, deveined and chopped
60 g (2 oz) vegetable oil
1 teaspoon salt and pepper mixture (see Salt and Pepper section)
1 shallot (spring onion/scallion), chopped
4 iceberg lettuce leaves, trimmed to rice bowl-sized cups
sesame oil, drizzle

Toast pine nuts by stirring them in a dry frying pan over medium heat for a few minutes, until they start to colour—watch them closely as they burn easily.

Bring a large saucepan of water to the boil. Add the prawns and when almost cooked, add the celery, water chestnuts, bamboo shoots and carrots. Drain very well.

Heat the oil in a wok over high heat, stir-fry the vegetables, prawns, salt and pepper mixture and a little sesame oil.

Stir in shallots and remove from heat.

Spoon the mixture into lettuce cups, sprinkle with pine nuts and serve.

Makes 4

Pickled Cucumber Garlic, Chilli and Rice Vinegar

This refreshing dish can be served on its own or accompanying any rice or noodle dish to give that extra texture to a dish

600 g (21 oz) Lebanese Cucumber, deseeded and cut into finger size
2 tablespoons salt,
6 cloves garlic, crushed, skin off
1 chilli, thinly sliced
1 teaspoon sugar
60 ml (2 fl oz) rice vinegar
Sesame oil, drizzle (added just before serving)

Marinade the cucumber with salt and set aside for 5 minutes. Rinse off the salt and drain well.

In a large mixing bowl, combine all ingredients and mix well, then place the bowl in the fridge for about 30 minutes, drizzle sesame oil and mix lightly to serve.

One serve

Crispy Pork Chop with Taiwanese Five Spice

1 kg (2.2 lb) pork chops (about 8–10 pieces)

Marinade
1 tablespoon soy sauce
1 teaspoon salt
½ teaspoon sugar
125 g (4 oz) potato flour
a pinch of cinnamon powder (see Basics)
1 whole egg
375 ml (12.5 fl oz) water

a pinch of Five Spice powder
2 teaspoon salt and pepper
Vegetable oil, for frying
500 g (16 oz) sweet potato powder, for coating the pork chop

Mix together 2 teaspoons of salt and pepper mixture with a pinch of five spice powder.

Use a meat tenderiser (pyramid hammer) to soften the pork chop and break the fibres apart.

Place all ingredients in a large mixing bowl and mix well then add the pork chop. Use hands to marinade and massage the pork chop for 10 minutes or until all marinade is absorb by the pork chop.

Dust the pork chop in a tray filled with the sweet potato powder. Rest the pork chop for 20 seconds before deep frying in a deep fryer at 170°C (340°F) for 3–4 minutes.

Cut the pork chop in to slices and serve with the Five Spice, salt and peper mixture on the side.

Makes enough for a party

Giblets with Shredded Ginger and Garlic Sauce

1 kg (2.2 lb) giblets, cleaned well
70 g (2.5 oz) salt
200 g (6.5 oz) ginger, sliced
5 stems shallots
small handful ginger, shredded, to serve

Sauce
1 tablespoon soy paste
2 cloves fresh garlic, minced
pinch of sugar
1 teaspoon water

To create the sauce, mix together the soy paste, minced garlic, sugar and water and mix well.

Blanch the giblets in boiling water. Drain and set aside.

Place all ingredients in a medium pot and fill with enough water to just cover the giblets. Bring the pot to boil, then simmer for 40 minutes.

Remove the giblets from the pot and cut into halves. Serve with the sauce and shredded ginger.

Makes enough for a party

Note
Leftover giblets should remain in the stock in fridge.
This dish is good to serve in all temperatures, hot, warm, room temperature, even cold! The textures are all different.

Calamari Salad with Taiwanese Garlic Five Spice Sauce

150 g (5 oz) calamari, cleaned, cross cut from inside in bite size pieces
2 large lettuce leaves, cut into large chunks
3 tablespoons Taiwanese Garlic Five Spice Sauce (see Sauces)

Bring water in a medium pot to boil, then add in the calamari to blanch quickly, for no more than 20 seconds. Remove calamari and drain.

Serve the calamari on a bed of lettuce or mixed leaf salad. Pour the sauce over the top of the calamari to serve.

One serve

> ### Note
> The cutting of calamari has to be done from inside for the calamari to curl up.

Braised Tofu with Ginger and Chilli Sauce

600 g (21 oz) tofu, cut into triangle shapes
600 ml (20 fl oz) water
125 ml (4 fl oz) soy sauce
2 teaspoon sugar
2 shallots, stemmed
3 cloves of garlic, skin on
Vegetable oil, for frying
Coriander, for garnish

Serving Sauce
2 tablespoon soy paste
1 teaspoon ginger, minced
1 teaspoon sugar
chilli, if preferred, minced

In a large pot, combine the water, soy sauce and sugar, and bring the pot to boil.

While it is boiling, deep fry the tofu, a few pieces at a time, until golden. Once cooked, move the tofu pieces into the pot of soy sauce and water. Towel dry the tofu to minimise oil spitting.

Deep fry the shallots and garlic until golden, and then add into the large pot with tofu.

Bring the large pot back to a boil, then simmer for 30 minutes.

Garnish with coriander to serve.

One serve

Note
If pork belly sauce is available, add a few table spoon to add more taste!

Potato Salad with Apple and Egg

200 g (6.5 oz) carrot, peeled and diced
200 g (6.5 oz) cucumber, peeled and diced
450 g (16 oz) potato, peeled and diced
500 g (1 lb) apple, peeled, deseeded and diced
200 g (6.5 oz) egg, boiled, peeled and diced
3 tablespoon salt
250 ml (8 fl oz) mayonnaise

In a large pot, boil the carrot and potato until it is cooked but still firm. Then drain well and place it in the fridge to cool.

Marinade the cucumber with salt and set aside for 10 minutes before rinsing and draining the cucumber.

Wash the apple with salt water to prevent apple from browning. Make sure that all of the ingredients are cold and that there is no excess water.

In a mixing bowl, combine all of the ingredients with Mayonnaise and mix well before serving.

One serve

Note
The Apple in the salad gives the extra crunch, and more refreshing than using onion. It's perfect over fresh baked bread or baguette.

Pickled Radish and Vegetables with Rice Vinegar

500g white radish, cut into diamond shapes, marinated with 2 teaspoon of
  salt
250g carrots, cut into diamond shapes, marinated with 1 teaspoon of salt
250g cucumber, deseeded, cut into diamonds, marinated in 1 teaspoon salt
1 long red chilli, deseeded, cut into diamond shape

300ml rice vinegar
200 g sugar

Marinate all the ingredients seperately as instructed for 5 minutes. Once marinated, wash off the salt and leave to stand in water for 5 minutes.

Drain the vegetables and mix with the rice vinegar and sugar and allow to marinate for 2 days before serving.

Makes enough for a party

Stewed Pigs Ear with Shredded Shallots and Sesame Oil

Stew
10 pigs ears, approximately 150 g (5 oz) each
3 shallots, stemmed
400 ml (13.5 fl oz)
6 pieces star anise
10 g (0.4 oz) rock sugar
25 g (0.9 oz) sugar
250 ml (8 fl oz) water
1 whole long chilli
8–10 cloves garlic, crushed with skin on

Serve
1 bunch shallots, half stemmed
1 small knob ginger, shredded
2 tablespoons soy paste
Chilli oil, optional
1 teaspoon sugar
Drizzle of sesame oil

Wash and clean pigs ear well.

In a large pot, combine all of the stew ingredients and top up with just enough water cover the pigs ears. Bring the pot to boil, then simmer for 30 minutes. Drain and put aside to cool.

To create the serving mixture, in a large bowl combine the shallots, ginger, soy sauce, chilli oil, sugar and sesame oil.

Once the ears have cooled, slice them thinly and mix well with serving mixture.

Makes enough for a party

String Beans with Fried Garlic

200 g string beans, cut into 5 cm (2 in) long pieces
1 teaspoon fried garlic, minced
1 teaspoon salt
1 tablespoon chilli, minced, optional

In a pot over medium heat, blanch the string beans for about 3 minutes, then remove and drain well.

In a mixing bowl, combine the string beans, fried garlic, salt and chilli (if preferred), and mix well. Ready to serve

One serve

Fried Garlic Mince

Peeled and minced fresh garlic, can be done manually or in a food processor.

Wash the minced garlic and drain as much excess water as possible.

In a wok on low heat, slowly fry the garlic, stirring constantly to avoid sticking and burning.

Once cooked and the garlic has turned golden brown, drain quickly.

The fried garlic can be prepared in bulk and stored in fridge for future use.

One serve

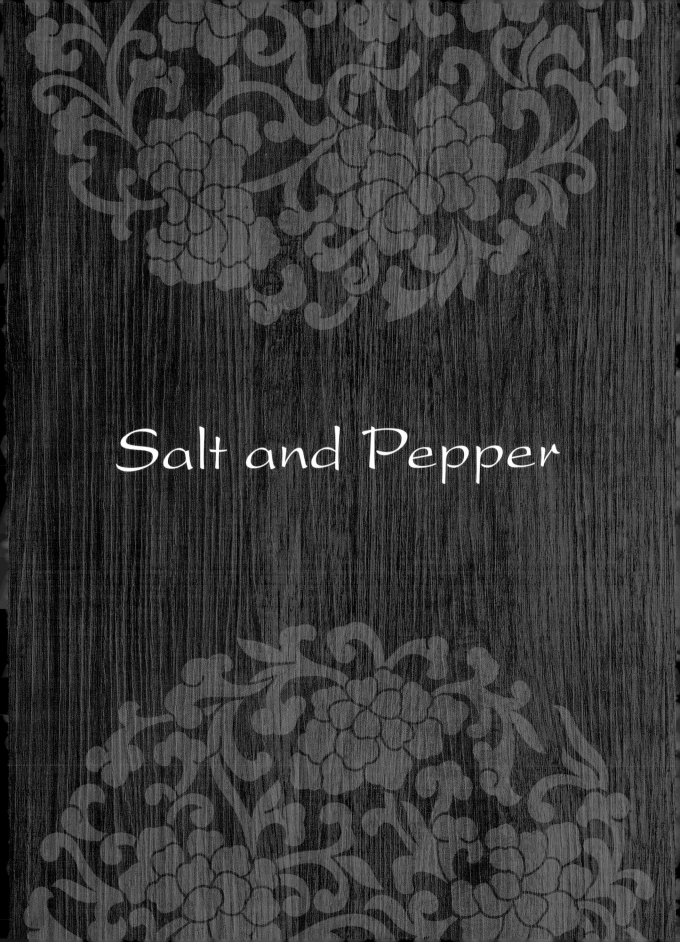

Salt and Pepper

Salt and Pepper Mixture

4 tablespoons salt
2 tablespoons sugar
1 tablespoon ground white pepper

Combine the salt, sugar and pepper in a spice grinder or mortar and pestle and mix until well blended.

When preparing large quantities, it is best to first wok toss the salt over low heat to remove any excess moisture.

Makes 1 cup

Note
Left over mixture can be stored in a well-sealed jar in a cool place (not refrigerated) for up to 3 months.

Salt and Pepper Squid

Salt and pepper dishes are very popular in Chinese and Taiwanese cuisine. There are several ways to do it. The process we use at blue eye dragon is simple, but the crucial steps of wok tossing must be done exactly right to get a perfect result!

Use as little oil as possible when tossing the shallots, garlic and chilli. You don't want any excess oil to be absorbed into the batter. A good trick is to use a spray vegetable oil, or rub a paper towel with a little oil on it over the wok.

1 whole squid
1 tablespoon salt and pepper mixture (see Salt and Pepper section)
vegetable oil, for deep-frying
250 ml (8 fl oz) cornflour
4–5 cloves garlic, finely sliced
1 long chilli, chopped (remove seeds if you want to minimise the spiciness)
2 shallots (spring onions/scallions), green section only, chopped

Clean the squid, cut the tubes open and cut a cross-hatch pattern into the insides. Be careful not to cut all the way through.

Cut the tubes into 4 x 2cm (2 x 1in) pieces and place in a mixing bowl with one pinch of the salt and pepper mixture, mix well.

Heat the oil in a deep fryer (or wok, see Basics) to 180°C (350°F).

Place the cornflour in a bowl and slowly add in enough water to make a batter with a consistency that is thicker than paint and slightly sticky. Then add in the squid. Use your whole hand to mix the squid with the batter, don't just coat the surface.

Slowly lower the squid into the hot oil, it should float when ready. Remove from the oil immediately.

Lightly oil a wok, place over high heat, throw in the garlic for a good stir and then the chilli and shallots. Finally add the squid, sprinkle with some of the salt and pepper mixture and give it all a good toss. Serve with some of the remaining mixture on the side.

One serve

Salt and Pepper Prawns

10 large fresh tiger prawns (shrimp), cleaned, deveined with tail on
1 tablespoon salt and pepper mixture (see Salt and Pepper section)
vegetable oil, for deep-frying
250 g (8 oz) cornflour
4–5 cloves garlic, finely sliced
1 long chilli, chopped (remove seeds if you want to minimise the spiciness)
2 shallots (spring onions/scallions), green section only, chopped

Place the prawns in a mixing bowl with one pinch of the salt and pepper mixture, mix well.

Heat the oil in a deep fryer (or wok, see Basics) to 180°C (350°F).

Put cornflour a bowl and slowly add in enough water to make a batter with a consistency that is thicker than paint and slightly sticky. Then add in the prawns. Use your whole hand to mix the prawns with the batter, don't just coat the surface.

Slowly lower the prawns into the hot oil, they should float when ready. Remove from the oil immediately.

Lightly oil a wok, turn on high heat, throw in the garlic for a good stir, and then the chilli and shallots. Finally add the prawns, sprinkle with some of the salt and pepper mixture and give it all a good toss. Serve with the remaining salt and pepper mixture on the side.

One serve

Salt and Pepper Soft Shell Crab

150 g (5 oz) soft shell crab
1 tablespoon salt and pepper mixture (see Salt and Pepper section)
vegetable oil, for deep-frying
250 g (8 oz) cornflour
4–5 cloves garlic, finely sliced
1 long chilli, chopped (remove seeds if you want to minimise the spiciness)
2 shallots (spring onions/scallions), green section only, chopped

Clean and cut each crab into 6 pieces. Place the crab pieces in a mixing bowl with one pinch of the salt and pepper mixture, mix well.

Heat the oil in a deep fryer (or wok, see Basics) to 180°C (350°F).

Put cornflour in the bowl with the crab pieces. Coat the crab pieces well, allow to rest for a minute. Shake off excess flour before deep-frying.

Slowly lower the crab pieces into the hot oil, they should float when ready. Remove from the oil immediately.

Lightly oil a wok, turn on high heat, throw in the garlic for a good stir, and then the chilli and shallots. Finally add the crab, sprinkle with some of the salt and pepper mixture and give it all a good toss. Serve with the remaining salt and pepper mixture on the side.

One serve

Salt and Pepper Tofu

vegetable oil, for deep-frying
250 g (8 oz) cornflour
tofu, cut into bite size pieces
4–5 cloves garlic, finely sliced
1 large chilli, deseeded and chopped
2 shallots (spring onions/scallions), chopped
½ tablespoon salt and pepper mixture (see Salt and Pepper section)

Heat the oil in a deep fryer (or wok, see Basics) to 180°C (350°F).

Put cornflour in a bowl and add the tofu. Gently coat the tofu and allow to rest for a minute.

Deep-fry until golden brown.

Lightly oil a wok, turn on high heat, throw in the garlic for a good stir, then the chilli and shallots.
Finally add the tofu, sprinkle with some of the salt and pepper mixture and give it all a good
toss. Serve with the remaining salt and pepper mixture on the side.

One serve

Salt and Pepper Whitebait

200 g (6½ oz) whitebait
1 tablespoon salt and pepper mixture (see Salt and Pepper section)
vegetable oil, for deep-frying
125 g (4 oz) cornflour
4–5 cloves garlic, finely sliced
1 large chilli, deseeded and chopped
2 shallots (spring onions/scallions), chopped

Wash and drain the whitebait well. Mix the whitebait with the cornflour in a mixing bowl. Remove the whitebait and shake off excess flour.

Heat the oil in a deep fryer (or wok, see Basics) to 180°C (350°F).

Deep-fry the whitebait and drain on a paper towel.

Lightly oil a wok, turn on high heat, throw in the garlic for a good stir, then the chilli and shallots. Finally add the whitebait, sprinkle with some of the salt and pepper mixture and give it all a good toss. Serve with the remaining salt and pepper mixture on the side.

One serve

Lightly Battered Fish Fillet with Salt and Pepper

200 g (6.5 oz) Basa fish fillet, cut to 2.5 cm (1 in) wide strips
2 tablespoons plain flour
a pinch salt
a pinch sugar
2 teaspoon Salt and Pepper mixture (see page 96)
250 g (8 oz) cornflour
Vegetable oil, for frying

In a bowl, marinade the fish pieces with salt and sugar, then set aside.

Mix together the plain flour with some water to form a lumpy consistency.

Place the marinated fish pieces in the flour mixture and coat well.

In a pan, heat vegetable oil to 180°C (350°F).

On a tray, dust the fish pieces with cornflour and let it rest for few seconds.

Place the fish pieces in the frypan and after about 3 minutes, they should begin to float. Drain on paper towel.

Sprinkle the Salt and Pepper mixture to the fish fillet, plate up and serve with remaining Salt and Pepper mixture.

One serve

Soups

Chicken Noodle Soup with Chinese Celery, Fried Shallots and Chinese Greens

1–2 stalks Chinese celery, finely chopped (see Glossary)
1 shallot, finely chopped
500 ml (8 fl oz) water (or chicken stock if available)
250 g (8 oz) chicken, cut into strips
500 g (8 oz) egg noodles
1 teaspoon salt
2 drops soy sauce
1 teaspoon sugar
ground white pepper, a pinch
½ tablespoon fried shallots (see Glossary)
Chinese greens

In a large pot, cook the noodles and then use the same pot to blanch the Chinese greens. Drain until ready to use.

In another pot, bring hot water/stock to the boil and put the chicken strips in for a few minutes until cooked.

Place the noodles in a bowl, top with the remaining ingredients and pour in the chicken and stock/water—the heat will release the flavours.

Garnish with coriander.

One serve

Note
If Chinese celery is unavailable you can use Western celery, but it will not have as much flavour. Mum always keeps trimmed excess chicken pieces (not presentable enough for stir-fries) to make chicken stock. Bring water to the boil, add the chicken pieces and simmer for 10 minutes.

Noodles with Minced Pork Sauce in Chicken Stock

Soup toppings
1–2 stalks Chinese celery, finely chopped (see glossary)
1 shallot, finely chopped
1 teaspoon of salt
1 teaspoon of sugar
Ground white pepper, a pinch
½ tablespoon of fried shallots (see glossary)

500 ml (16 fl oz) of water or Chicken stock if available
100 g (3.5 oz) dry noodles or 200 g (7 oz fresh noodles
Chinese greens
3 tablespoon of minced pork sauce

In a large pot, cook the noodles until soft and and then use the same pot to blanch the Chinese greens.

Drain well and place noodles and chinese greens in a serving bowl. Add the chinese celery, shallot, salt, sugar, pepper and fried shallots in to the bowl.

In another pot, bring water or chicken stock to boil, and pour this mixture over the noodles and ingredients. The heat will release all the flavours.

Pour the minced pork sauce on top and garnish with Chinese greens and coriander to serve.

One serve

Chicken and Vegetable Soup with Egg Noodles

100 g (4 oz) chicken, cut into strips
2 tablespoons cornflour
vegetable oil, for deep-frying
500 g (16 oz) egg noodles, cooked
2 Chinese mushrooms, soften in hot water and cut into strips
60 g (2 oz) carrot, shredded into strips
bamboo shoots
100 g (4 oz) enoki mushrooms
200g (7oz) Chinese cabbage, cut into strips

Seasoning
1½ teaspoon salt
1 teaspoon bonito powder (see Glossary)
½ teaspoon sugar
½ tablespoon soy sauce
1 tablespoon black vinegar (see Glossary)
ground white pepper, a pinch
1 tablespoon potato flour mixed with 1 tablespoon water to make a paste
  (see Glossary)
coriander, (cilantro) to serve

Marinate the chicken in the cornflour thoroughly. Heat oil in the wok and deep-fry the chicken until crispy. Drain on paper towels.

Bring 750 ml (13.5 fl oz) water to the boil and add the vegetables. Bring back to the boil and add all seasoning and chicken. Thicken with potato paste.

Place noodles in a bowl and cover with the vegetable soup to serve.

One serve

> Note
> Replace chicken with pork if preferred.
> Traditionally in Taiwan, families use pork.

Chicken Huntun (Wonton) Soup

Filling
250 g (8 oz) minced chicken
sugar, salt and pepper, a pinch each
2 teaspoons potato flour (see
  Glossary)
1 tablespoon water
1 packet of huntun (wonton) pastry
  (see Glossary)

Soup seasoning
1 teaspoon salt
1 teaspoon sugar
ground white pepper, a pinch
2 drops soy sauce
1 shallot, finely chopped
½ tablespoon fried shallots (see
  Glossary)
1 stalk coriander (cilantro), chopped
Chinese greens
500 ml (16 fl oz) chicken stock/water

Mix the chicken together with the salt, pepper, sugar, potato flour and water.

Stir until the water is absorbed into the chicken.

Place one teaspoon of chicken mince in the centre of a huntun pastry. Spread the mixture out over two-thirds of the pastry. Spreading out the filling means a pocket of air is left inside the pastry which makes them float.

Gather the edges of the pastry at the top. Pinch and twist to seal the top. Repeat with the rest of the pastry and mince.

Bring a pot of water to the boil.

Place the huntuns in the boiling water, stirring occasionally to avoid them sticking to the pot. Once they float to the surface, wait a further two minutes, then drain them and put into a serving bowl.

Use the same pot to blanch the Chinese greens. Drain and discard the water.

Boil the stock/water for the soup. Put all the soup seasoning over the huntuns in a bowl. Pour the soup over the huntuns and garnish with coriander.

One serve

Chicken Soup with Ginger, Wolfberries, Rice Wine and Sesame Oil

There is no water in this recipe at all. It is traditional in Taiwan to make this soup as an important daily meal, for a woman in the first month after she has given birth. It is believed that this will restore her to good health. It is full of nutrients and considered very warming—especially good if you feel cold and shivery!

500 g (1 lb) chicken thigh
1 tablespoon Chinese wolfberries (see Glossary)
60 ml (2 fl oz) black sesame oil
50 g (2 oz) ginger, sliced
600 ml (20 fl oz) rice wine
salt, a pinch
½ tablespoon sugar

Cut chicken into 2–3 cm (¼ in) cubes.

Soak wolfberries in water to soften, then drain.

Heat wok over high heat. Add sesame oil and stir-fry the ginger until slightly dry and fragrant.

Toss in the chicken and stir-fry until almost cooked through.

Pour in half of the rice wine and bring to the boil. Be very careful as there is a danger of it catching fire – the rice wine is highly flammable.

Add the wolfberries and turn the heat down to medium, then add the other half of the rice wine.

Simmer for a few minutes until the chicken is fully cooked. Add the salt and sugar.

One serve

Taiwanese Traditional Beef Noodle Soup

This makes extra beef and stock. Freeze them separately and defrost them both when needed. Pour them over some noodles and you have a very quick and tasty meal.

2 kg (4 lb) beef brisket
1 tablespoon sesame oil
60 g (2 oz) ginger, sliced
1 shallot (spring onion/scallion)
3 cloves garlic, minced
1 tablespoon star anise
3 teaspoons sugar
¼ tablespoon Szechuan peppercorns (see Glossary)
2 teaspoons chilli bean sauce (see Glossary)
3.75 litre (8 pint) water
750 ml (25 fl oz) soy sauce

1 tablespoon white rock sugar (see Glossary)

To serve
1 bunch spinach (silverbeet)
500 g (16 oz) cooked white noodles
sesame oil, to drizzle
1 shallot (spring onion, scallion), finely chopped
1 stalk coriander (cilantro)
A few stalks of Chinese greens
chilli oil, to taste (optional—see Glossary)

Blanch the beef for 1 minute to make it easier to cut. Trim off most of the fat and cut it into 2cm (¾in) cubes.

Heat up the wok over high heat, add the sesame oil and stir-fry the ginger, garlic, star anise and Szechuan peppercorns until fragrant.

Add the sugar, chilli bean sauce, water, soy sauce and white rock sugar. Check at this point that it tastes a little bit salty. Add the beef.

Simmer for 80 minutes with the lid on. Remove beef and set aside. Sieve the liquid for the soup and reserve.

Blanch the Chinese greens. Place the noodles, Chinese greens and beef in a bowl and pour over enough soup to cover.

Drizzle with sesame oil, garnish with shallots and coriander or chilli oil to serve.

One serve

Combination Vegetable Soup with Crispy Fried Eggs

2 Chinese dried mushrooms
750 ml (25 fl oz) water
5 pieces (250 g/8 oz) Chinese cabbage, cut into strips
60 g (2 oz) enoki mushrooms
60 g (2 oz) carrots, cut into strips
1½ teaspoons salt
½ teaspoon sugar
1 teaspoon bonito powder (see Glossary)
125 g (4 oz) vegetable oil
1 egg, lightly beaten
1 tablespoon potato flour mixed with 1 tablespoon water to make a paste
  (see Glossary)
500 g (16 oz) egg noodles, cooked
coriander (cilantro), to serve

Soften the dried mushrooms in a little water then drain, discard stalks and slice the caps into strips.

Heat the oil in a wok over high heat. Add the egg and stir with chopsticks in a circular motion until the egg is slightly set.

Lower the heat to medium—this is very important otherwise the egg will not cook through evenly. Slowly stir-fry until it smells like a cake and separates into strips.

Use the same wok and oil to quickly stir-fry the mushrooms until fragrant.

In a pot, bring water to the boil, add mushrooms, all the vegetables and seasoning, then bring back to the boil. Add the egg strips, stir quickly and mix in the flour paste to thicken.

Place noodles in a bowl and cover them with the soup.

Garnish with the coriander.

One serve

Beef, Tofu and Vegetables Soup

150 g (5 oz) tofu, cut into cubes
50 g (2 oz) carrots diced, blanched and drained
50 g (2 oz) celery, diced
50 g (2 oz) water chestnuts (can be canned), diced
50 g (2 oz) mushrooms, diced
150 g (5 oz) beef, diced and marinated
Water
2 egg whites
Potato flour mixed with water, for thickening
1 tablespoon salt, to season
Pepper, to enhance flavour if preferred

Marinate the beef with 2 tablespoons of water, a pinch of salt and pepper and 1 tablespoon of potato flour. Boil the water, add all ingredients except tofu and bring the pot to boil.

Add tofu for another quick boil and season with salt and pepper.

Bring the pot to the boil again, then turn the heat down and use potato flour water to thicken the soup, mix to desire thickness.

Beat up the egg white, stir the soup in circular motion while poring the egg white slowly to the soup. Turn of the heat right away.

This soup is fairly light, will require a little bit more salt if serving over rice or noodle.

One serve

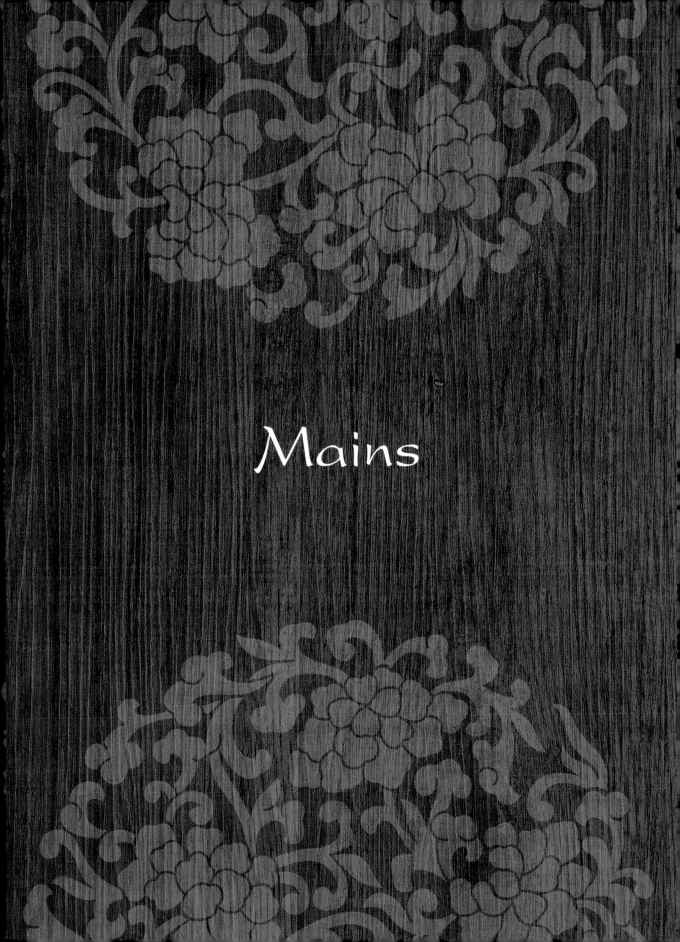

Mains

Pork Belly

2.5 kg (5 lb) pork belly, skin on
400 ml (13 fl oz) soy sauce
2 shallots (spring onions/scallions)
5 cloves garlic, with skin off
3–4 pieces star anise
2 tablespoons sugar
½ tablespoon white rock sugar (see Glossary)
1 small chilli, whole
coriander (cilantro), to serve

Wash the pork belly and clean the skin with a knife. Mum always says she's giving the pork a good shave! Dry well with paper towels or a tea towel. Cut into 3 cm (1 in) cubes.

Spread the cubes out on an oven tray and place under the grill to quickly brown all sides. Traditionally, Mum would deep-fry the pork until golden but this can mean lots of wasted oil.

Put the pork belly and soy sauce in a large pan over high heat.

Stir thoroughly until the pork belly absorbs the soy sauce evenly (about 2 mintues). Then add enough water to just cover the meat, followed by the shallots, garlic, star anise, sugar and chilli.

Bring to the boil, then cook over medium heat—slightly higher than simmer, for 40–50 minutes without the lid on and stirring constantly.

For a softer texture, simmer for an extra 5 minutes, otherwise serve in a bowl and garnish with coriander.

Remove chilli and shallots before serving.

One serve

> **Note**
> This makes more than one serve. Freeze unused portions and reheat as required. Do not reduce the sauce too much, or it will be too salty.

Stir-fried Vermicelli with Pork, Vegetables, Dried Shrimp and Black Vinegar

3 dried Chinese mushrooms
1 tablespoon dried shrimp
60 ml (2 fl oz) vegetable oil
200 g (7 oz) pork, cut into thin 5 cm
  (2 in) strips
250 g (8 oz) onion, cut into strips
125 g (4 oz) carrot, cut into strips
1 shallot (spring onion/scallion), cut
  to match the size of the carrot
2 leaves savoy cabbage, shredded
350 g (11 oz) cooked vermicelli, (100
  g (4 oz) precooked)

Seasoning
ground white pepper, a pinch
2 tablespoons soy sauce
1 teaspoon sugar
1 teaspoon black vinegar (see
  Glossary)
125 ml (4 fl oz) water
½ teaspoon salt

Soften the mushrooms in water. Drain, remove stalks and slice the caps. Soften the dried shrimp in water. Drain.

Heat up the wok over high heat. Add the oil, stir-fry the pork until almost cooked, then add the onion and stir-fry until soft. Add carrots, shallots, shrimp and cabbage and stir-fry for 1 minute.

Combine the seasoning ingredients and pour into the wok.

Lastly, add the cooked noodles and stir-fry on medium heat until they have absorbed the liquid, and taken on the colour of the seasoning. The noodle should taste a little bit chewy and elastic-like.

One serve

> Note
> Quality of the vermicelli determines how well this dish tastes.

Taiwanese Sweet and Sour Pork Ribs

350 g (11 oz) pork ribs, cut into 4–5 cm (1½–2 in) cubes
1 teaspoon soy sauce
sugar, a pinch
salt, a pinch
½ egg, lightly beaten
250 g (8 oz) cornflour
vegetable oil, for deep frying
½ onion, cut into strips
2 tablespoons Taiwanese Sweet and Sour Sauce (see Sauces)
1 shallot (spring onion, scallion), washed and finely sliced/shredded, to
  garnish
1 long chilli, finely sliced/shredded, to garnish
vegetable oil, 1 tablespoon

Marinate the pork in the salt, sugar and egg for 10 minutes.

Place the cornflour in a bowl, add the pork and use your hands to make sure the pork is well coated.

Shake off excess flour and leave meat to rest.

Heat the oil in a deep fryer (or wok, see Basics) to 180°C (350°F). Add the pork a few pieces at a time and deep- fry for 3–4 minutes or until crispy.

As you remove each batch from the oil, drain it on paper towels.

Clean the wok, add 1 tablespoon of oil and lightly fry the onion until soft and fragrant.

Return the pork to the wok and add the Sweet and Sour Sauce, making sure all the ingredients are well coated. Garnish with finely sliced shredded shallots and chilli.

One serve

Note
Taiwanese sweet and sour sauce uses black vinegar
which gives a different taste. Replace pork ribs with lean
pork if preferred.

Stewed Beef Brisket with Spinach

2 kg (4 lb) beef brisket
1 tablespoon sesame oil
60 g (oz) ginger, sliced
2 shallot (spring onion/scallion),
   whole
3 cloves garlic, minced
1 tablespoon star anise
3 teaspoons sugar
¼ tablespoon Szechuan
   peppercorns
2 teaspoons chilli bean sauce (see
Glossary)
3.75 litre (8 pint) water
750 ml (25 fl oz) soy sauce
1 tablespoon white rock sugar (see
   Glossary)
1 bunch spinach (silverbeet)
½ tomato, cut into cubes
1 shallot (spring onion, scallion) cut
   into 2–3 cm (¾–1½ in) pieces
½ teaspoon potato flour (see
   Glossary)

Blanch the beef for 1 minute to make it easier to cut. Trim off most of the fat and cut it into 2cm (¾in) cubes.

Heat up the wok over high heat, add the sesame oil and stir-fry the ginger, garlic, star anise and Szechuan peppercorns until fragrant.

Add the sugar, shallots, chilli bean sauce, water, soy sauce and white rock sugar. Check at this point that it tastes a little bit salty. Add the beef.

Simmer for 80 minutes with the lid on.

Remove beef from the wok and set aside.

Sieve the liquid and reserve.

Combine potato flour with ½ teaspoon of water to make a paste.

In a separate wok, take ½ cup of the liquid, add tomato, shallots and 250 g (8 oz) of beef. Add potato paste to thicken.

Blanch the spinach, drain well. Place spinach on a plate and spoon the beef and sauce over it.

One serve

> **Note**
> You can freeze the rest of the liquid and beef for later use in beef noodle soup.

Ginger Shallot Beef

250g (8oz) beef skirt, thinly sliced against the grain
1 tablespoon soy sauce
½ teaspoon sugar
potato flour, a pinch (see Glossary)
60 ml (2fl oz) vegetable oil
125 g (4 oz) ginger, thinly sliced
6 green shallots (spring onions/scallions), cut in 2–3 cm (¾ in) pieces
1 long chilli, thinly sliced at an angle

Marinate the beef with a drop of soy sauce, a drop of water, a pinch of sugar and potato flour. Mix well, then add a teaspoon of oil for a further mix.

Heat the wok to very hot before adding the remaining oil. Stir-fry the ginger until fragrant and then add the beef and quickly stir-fry.

Once the beef begins to change colour, add the shallots to the wok and stir. Finally, add the remaining soy sauce and sugar, mix through, remove from the heat and serve.

One serve

Beef in Taiwanese BBQ Sauce with Spinach

Marinade
1 teaspoon soy sauce
sugar, a pinch
1 teaspoon potato flour (see Glossary)
½ tablespoon water
1 tablespoon vegetable oil

250 g (8 oz) beef skirt
1½ tablespoons Taiwanese BBQ sauce (see Glossary)
250 g (8 oz) spinach (silverbeet), cut into 5 cm (2 in) strips
2 tablespoons vegetable oil
2 cloves garlic, sliced
1 chilli, deseeded and cut at an angle
½ tablespoon soy sauce

Combine the marinade ingredients.

Thinly slice the beef against the grain and mix with the marinade for a few minutes.

Mix in the BBQ sauce.

Blanch spinach in water and drain.

Heat up the wok over high heat, add the oil and stir-fry the beef until almost done.

Add the garlic and chilli to the wok, stir then add in the soy sauce. Stir-fry until the meat is cooked.

Place the spinach on a plate and top with the beef to serve.

One serve

> **Note**
> Taiwanese BBQ sauce can be purchased from Asian grocery stores. Spinach can be replaced with other Chinese greens, such as water spinach or Chinese broccoli.

Chicken Fried Rice

150 g (5 oz) chicken breasts, cut into thin 5 cm (2 in) strips
½ teaspoon salt
½ teaspoon sugar
1 teaspoon cornflour
2 tablespoons vegetable oil
500 g (16 oz) steamed rice
2 eggs
¼ medium onion, diced
¼ medium carrot, diced and cooked
60 g (2 oz) diced shallot (spring onion/scallion), green end only
½ tablespoon soy sauce
ground white pepper, a pinch

To marinate the chicken, mix with a pinch of salt, sugar, cornflour, and some vegetable oil. Leave for 10 minutes.

Heat the wok to almost smoking, add some oil to moisten the wok, then add the eggs. Stir-fry the eggs until scrambled into pieces. Remove them from the wok when well done.

Use the same wok to stir-fry the chicken. When the chicken is almost cooked, add onions and carrots for a quick stir, then add the rice. Mix all together until the rice is heated through, then return the egg back to the wok.

Sprinkle the remaining salt, sugar and pepper over the rice and stir.

Drizzle with soy sauce and add chopped shallots for a final stir.

One serve

Note
Add ingredients to your liking, fried rice is all about what's available in the fridge. The most important part of the process is heating the wok before cooking. This will improve the texture of the fried eggs and the rice. The green end of shallots add colour to the fried rice.

Sanbei Chicken with Basil

250 g (8 oz) chicken fillet, cut in 2–3 cm (¾ in) cubes
60 ml (2fl oz) sesame oil
60 g (2 oz) ginger, sliced
4 cloves garlic, sliced
2 shallots (spring onions/scallions), cut into 2cm (¾in) slices
1 chilli, chopped
2 tablespoons soy sauce
1 tablespoon soy paste (see Glossary)
2 tablespoons rice wine
2 tablespoons sugar
250 g (8 oz) basil leaves

Heat up the wok over high heat, add the sesame oil and stir-fry the ginger for about 15–20 seconds.

Add the garlic and chicken to the wok and stir-fry until golden. Then add the shallots and chilli for a further stir.

Add soy sauce, paste, wine and sugar and stir-fry until the sauce is reduced.

Quickly stir through the basil then transfer to a plate and serve.

One serve

> ### Note
> If you have a cast iron bowl, heat up the bowl on the gas stove or in the oven to produce the sizzling effect when you serve. Traditionally in Taiwan, chicken maryland is used for this dish, and some use a whole chicken also.

Ginger Shallot Chicken

60 ml (2 fl oz) vegetable oil
125 ml (4 fl oz) ginger, cut into thin strips
250 g (8 oz) chicken, cut into thin 5cm (2ins) strips
6 green shallots (spring onions/scallions), cut in 2–3 cm (¾ in) pieces
½ teaspoon salt
½ teaspoon sugar
1 long chilli, thinly sliced at an angle (deseeded if you want to minimise the
  spiciness)

Heat the wok to very hot before adding the oil. Stir-fry the ginger until fragrant, then add the chicken and quickly stir-fry.

Once the chicken begins to change colour, add the shallots to the wok and stir. Finally, add the salt, sugar and chilli, mix through, remove from heat and serve.

One serve

Soy Paste Chicken
with Shredded Shallots

250 g (8 oz) chicken, cut into thin 5 cm (2 in) strips
½ teaspoon salt
½ teaspoon sugar
60 ml (2 fl oz) vegetable oil
2 tablespoons soy paste (see Glossary)

Topping
6 green shallots (spring onions/scallions), finely sliced
1 red chilli, deseeded and finely sliced

Marinate the chicken with the salt and sugar.

Wash the shallots and chilli after slicing to produce the curling effect, and to minimise the sharpness of the shallots.

Heat the wok to very hot and add the oil. Stir-fry the chicken until cooked through, then stir in soy paste and cook for a few seconds.

Transfer chicken onto a plate with shallots and chilli on top.

Mix together when serving at the table.

One serve

Chilli Curry Chicken

80 ml (2½ fl oz) vegetable oil
250 g (8 oz) chicken, cut into cubes
½ onion, cut into bite-sized pieces
1½ tablespoons curry powder
3 snow peas
60 g (2 oz) capsicum (sweet pepper/bell pepper), cut into bite-sized pieces
1 chilli, chopped (add more if you like it hot)
¼ teaspoon salt
¾ teaspoon sugar
60 ml (2 fl oz) water
1 teaspoon of potato flour (see Glossary)

Heat the wok over high heat and add the oil. Once hot, stir-fry the chicken until cooked, then remove from the wok.

In the same wok, stir-fry the onion until soft and fragrant, then add the curry powder and stir through.

Toss in the snow peas, capsicum, chilli, salt and sugar for a quick stir-fry before pouring in the water.

Combine the potato flour with 1 teaspoon of water to make a paste.

Once the sauce comes to the boil, stir in the potato paste to thicken then serve.

One serve

Chicken in Kong-Bao Sauce

250 g (8 oz) chicken, cut into 2–3 cm (¾ in) cubes

Marinade
salt, a pinch
sugar, a pinch
1 teaspoon vegetable oil

1 teaspoon potato flour (see Glossary)
60 ml (2 fl oz) vegetable oil
60 ml (2 fl oz) ginger
60 g (2 oz) dried chillies
3 green shallots (spring onions/scallions), cut in 2–3cm (¾in) pieces
60 ml (2 fl oz) Kong-Bao Sauce (see Sauces)

Mix the chicken with the salt and sugar, then when well combined mix in the oil.

Heat the wok over high heat then add the oil. When the oil is hot, add the chicken and quickly stir-fry until cooked. Remove from the wok.

In the same wok, add the ginger and stir-fry until fragrant, then add the dried chilli and shallots for a minute. Return the chicken to the wok and stir through the Kong-Bao sauce and serve.

One serve

Prawn Omelette

10 large green prawns (shrimp), peeled and deveined
¼ teaspoon salt
¼ teaspoon sugar
1 teaspoon cornflour
125 ml (4 fl oz) vegetable oil

Omelette mixture
5 large eggs
¼ teaspoon salt
½ teaspoon sugar
1 teaspoon potato flour (see Glossary)
2 shallots (spring onions/scallions), finely chopped

Combine the prawns with the salt, sugar and cornflour. Mix well, and then mix in 1 tablespoon of the oil.

To make the omelette mixture, lightly beat eggs with salt and sugar, set aside.

Combine the potato flour with 3 teaspoons of water to make a paste and whisk into the omelette mixture.

Heat a wok, add 80 ml (2.5 fl oz) of oil and stir-fry the prawns over high heat for 2–3 minutes, or until they've just changed colour and curled up.

Add the omelette mixture, stir, then turn the heat back to medium and continue stirring the mixture gently until the eggs set.

Pour the remaining oil around the outside edge of the omelette to prevent it sticking, lift the edges and slide it onto a plate to serve.

One serve

Garlic Prawns with Shallots and Fish Sauce

12 large green prawns (shrimp), deveined but not peeled
10 cloves garlic, finely chopped
2 shallots (spring onions/scallions), finely chopped
250 ml (8 fl oz) vegetable oil
125 ml (4 fl oz) Fish Sauce, heated (see Sauces)

On a plate place the prawns open side up and sprinkle the garlic evenly over the top.

Start up the steamer, when the water is boiling place the plate of prawns in and steam for about 3 minutes over medium heat. The time will depend on the size of the prawns—as a rule when the prawns turn red they are almost done.

Remove the prawns from the steamer, place on a clean plate and sprinkle with the shallots.

Heat up the oil in a wok until almost smoking and drizzle the oil evenly over the plate. Repeat with the fish sauce and serve

One serve

Ginger Shallot Prawns

8 king prawns (shrimp), peeled and deveined, heads and tails on
sugar, a pinch,
ground white pepper, a pinch
1 teaspoon potato flour (see Glossary)
60 ml (2 fl oz) vegetable oil
60 ml (2 fl oz) ginger, sliced
6 shallots (spring onions/scallions), cut into 5cm (2ins) pieces
¼ red capsicum (sweet pepper/bell pepper), cut into diamond-shaped strips
4 snow peas (mange tout/sugar peas)
4 button mushrooms, cut in half
1 teaspoon sugar
1 teaspoon salt

Marinate the prawns in the pepper and sugar for a few minutes.

Combine the potato flour with 1 teaspoon of water to make a paste.

Heat the wok over high heat, add the oil and stir-fry the ginger until golden.

Add shallots and prawns to stir until almost cooked. Then add all the vegetables and stir-fry.

Mix in the sugar and salt, then stir in the potato paste to thicken the sauce.

Serve.

One serve

Prawns in Jade's Bloody Plum Sauce

125 ml (4 fl oz) vegetable oil
25 g (0.9 oz) dry vermicelli noodles/green bean noodle
8 large king prawns (shrimp), peeled and deveined, heads off and tails on
sugar, a pinch
ground white pepper, a pinch
1 tablespoon cornflour
vegetable oil for deep-frying
60 ml (2 fl oz) Plum Sauce (see Sauces)
salt, a pinch

Heat the wok over high heat, add the oil and fry the noodles until white and crispy. Drain them on paper towels and set aside to cool down.

Marinate the prawns in the sugar and pepper for a few minutes.

Coat the prawns in the cornflour, let it rest for a few minutes.

Heat the oil in a deep fryer (or wok, see Basics) to 180°C (350°F).

Fry the prawns in batches, when they float to the surface they're cooked. Remove them immediately and drain on paper towels.

Pour the plum sauce into a lightly oiled wok over high heat to reduce the sauce, then return the prawns to the wok and toss well to coat evenly.

Serve the prawns on a bed of the deep-fried noodles.

One serve

Sweet and Sour Fish Fillets

250g (8oz) white fish fillets, cut in to 2x5x1cm (¾x2x½in) pieces
salt, a pinch
sugar, a pinch
½ egg, lightly beaten
250 g (8 oz) cornflour
vegetable oil, for deep-frying
¼ onion, cut into 2cm (¾in) cubes
¼ red capsicum (sweet pepper/bell pepper), cut into 2cm (¾in) diamond-
  shaped strips
a few snowpeas
2 pineapple rings, cut to match the size of the capsicum
125ml (4 fl oz) Sweet and Sour Sauce (see Sauces)

Marinate fish in the salt, sugar and egg for a few minutes.

Place the cornflour in a bowl, add the fish and use your hands to make sure the fish is well coated.

Shake off excess flour and leave to rest.

Heat the wok over high heat then add the oil. When the oil is hot, add the fish a few pieces at a time and deep-fry for 3–4 minutes till crispy.

As you remove each batch from the oil, drain it on paper towels.

Clean wok, add 1 tablespoon of oil and lightly fry the onion until soft and fragrant. Add in the snowpeas, capsicum and pineapple and stir.

Pour the Sweet and Sour Sauce for a further stir, then return the fish to the wok to toss well and evenly.

One serve

Pan-Fried Snapper with Ginger, Soy, Chilli and Shallots

1 whole 500 g (1 lb) snapper, cleaned
125 ml (4 fl oz) vegetable oil
60 g (2 oz) ginger strips
2 shallots (spring onions/scallions), chopped
1 long chilli, cut at an angle
2 tablespoon soy sauce
1 tablespoon water
1 teaspoon sugar

Cut 3 slashes into the skin on each side of the snapper.

Heat the wok over high heat, add the oil and pan-fry the fish until golden brown on both sides.

Turn the heat to low and continue to cook the fish until tender—you can tell it's done if you can easily insert a chopstick into the flesh.

Push the fish to one side of the wok and stir-fry the ginger until softened, then toss in the shallots, chilli and soy sauce. Cook for a few seconds.

Turn the fish to coat it in the sauce, then add the water and sugar to finish.

Place the fish on a serving plate and pour over the sauce.

One serve

Sanbei Calamari with Basil

250 g (8 oz) calamari, cleaned, skin on and cut into 1cm (½in) rings
60 g (2 oz) ginger, sliced
2 tablespoons soy sauce
1 tablespoon soy paste (see Glossary)
2 tablespoons sugar
4 cloves garlic, sliced
2 shallots (spring onions/scallions), chopped into 2cm (¾in) slices
1 long chilli, chopped
60 ml (2 fl oz) sesame oil
2 tablespoons rice wine
250 g (8 oz) basil leaves

Quickly blanch the calamari in a pot of boiling water—be careful not to overcook the calamari at this stage. Drain very well.

Heat the wok over high heat, add the oil and stir-fry the ginger until fragrant.

Add the garlic and calamari to the wok and stir-fry until golden. Then add the shallots and chilli for a further stir.

Add soy sauce, paste, wine and sugar and stir-fry until the sauce is reduced.

Quickly stir through the basil then transfer to a plate and serve.

One serve

Note
If you have a cast iron bowl, heat up the bowl on the gas
stove or in the oven to produce the sizzling effect when
you serve.

Spicy Turban Shells with Garlic and Basil in Seafood Sauce

10 turban shells
60 ml (2 fl oz) vegetable oil
1 shallot (spring onion/scallion) cut into 2–3 cm (¾–1 in) pieces
1 clove garlic, minced
1 long chilli, sliced
2 tablespoons Seafood Sauce (see Sauces)
60 g (2 oz) basil leaves
sesame oil, to drizzle
2 iceberg lettuce cups

Bring a large pot of water to the boil and blanch the turban shells for about 1 minute. Drain and remove the meat from the shells, trimming off the hard part of the meat. Thinly slice.

Heat the wok over high heat, add the oil then the shallots, garlic and chilli. Stir well, then add the turban shell meat and Seafood Sauce and stir again briefly.

Add basil and sesame oil and mix thoroughly to finish.

Serve into two lettuce cups.

One serve

Scallops in XO Sauce

10 fresh scallops, roe and shell off
sugar, a pinch
cornflour, a pinch
1 teaspoon potato flour (see Glossary)
3 tablespoons vegetable oil
4 cloves garlic, sliced
2 shallots (spring onion/scallion), cut into 2–3 cm (¾ in) strips
1 long chilli, sliced at an angle
a few snow peas (mange tout/sugar peas)
¼ capsicum (sweet pepper/bell pepper) cut into diamond-shaped strips
2 tablespoons XO Sauce (see Glossary)
1 teaspoon sugar
1 teaspoon water

Marinate the scallops in a pinch of sugar and cornflour.

Combine the potato flour with 1 teaspoon of water to make a paste.

Heat the wok over high heat, add the oil and then stir-fry the scallops until they look plump. Remove from the wok.

In the same wok, stir-fry the garlic, shallots and chilli until fragrant, then add the snow peas and capsicums. Mix together, add the XO sauce, sugar and water and the return the scallops to the wok.

Stir in the potato paste to thicken the sauce then serve.

One serve

Ginger Shallot Calamari

350 g (11 oz) calamari, cleaned, skin on and cut into 1cm (½in) rings
1 teaspoon potato flour (see Glossary)
2 tablespoons vegetable oil
60 g (2 oz) ginger, cut into thin strips
6 shallots (spring onions/scallions), cut into 5cm (2ins) pieces
1 chilli, cut at an angle
½ teaspoon sugar
¼ teaspoon salt

Quickly blanch the calamari in a pot of boiling water—be careful not to overcook the calamari at this stage. Drain very well.

Combine the potato flour with 1 teaspoon of water to make a paste.

Heat the wok over high heat, add the oil and stir-fry the ginger until golden.

Add shallots and chilli and stir-fry.

Mix in the sugar and salt, then the calamari and stir in the potato paste to thicken the sauce.

Serve.

One serve

Seafood Congee

This recipe gives you a softer texture than a regular risotto. If you prefer to have your congee almost soup-like, add a bit more hot water before adding the seafood.

250 g (8 oz) rice
2.25 litre (5 pint) water
ginger, few slices
1 small fish fillet, cut into 6 pieces
6 large green prawns (shrimp), deveined and halved
1 calamari, cleaned and cut into rings
6 scallops, roe off

Seasoning
1 teaspoon salt
1 teaspoon bonito powder (see Glossary)
ground white pepper, a pinch

2 shallots (spring onions/scallions), finely chopped
1 stick celery, finely chopped (or Chinese celery if available—see Glossary)

Wash rice well and drain.

Bring rice, water and ginger to the boil in a large pot, stirring constantly to avoid the rice from sticking to the pot. Once the water is boiled, turn the heat down to a simmer and cook the rice without a lid.

Meanwhile, use another pot of boiling water to blanch the seafood quickly. Drain.

Once the rice is cooked, and the water is significantly reduced, add the seafood and seasoning and bring back to the boil. Remove the pot from the heat.

Add the shallots and celery to the congee, mix well and serve.

One serve

> Note
> You can add any variety of seafood you like, just be careful not to overcook it.

Tofu Stuffed with Minced Pork and Prawn in Black Pepper Sauce

Stuffing
250 g (8 oz) minced (ground) pork
60 g (2 oz) minced (ground) prawn
¼ shallot (spring onion/scallion), finely chopped
½ teaspoon Chinese celery, finely chopped (see Glossary)
ground white pepper, a pinch
sugar, a pinch
salt, a pinch
1 teaspoon sesame oil
½ tablespoon water
1 tablespoon potato flour (see Glossary)

10 pieces of tofu, cut into 3x5x1.5cm (1½x2x½ in) pieces
250 ml (8 fl oz) vegetable oil, for deep-frying
125 ml (4 fl oz) soy paste (see Glossary)
black pepper, a pinch
½ teaspoon sugar
½ tablespoon water
10 shallots (spring onions/scallions), green part only
½ teaspoon potato flour

Combine the potato flour with ½ teaspoon of water to make paste.

Thoroughly combine the stuffing ingredients.

Make a hole in the middle of each piece of tofu and fill with the mixture. Pack as much into each one for a tight fit.

Steam over boiling water for 10 minutes. Let it cool before deep frying.

Heat the oil in a deep fryer (or wok, see Basics) to 180°C (350°F).

Deep-fry the tofu in batches, until crispy on the outside. Drain on paper towels.

Mix together the water, soy paste, black pepper and sugar, then add the tofu.

Bring the sauce to the boil then thicken with the potato paste. Serve on hot plate with shallots across to prevent the tofu from sticking on the plate.

One serve

Garlic Tofu with Minced Chicken

500 ml (16 fl oz) vegetable oil, to fry tofu
1 tablespoon vegetable oil
tofu, cut in 2 cm (¾ in) cubes, do not use silken tofu or hard tofu
½ teaspoon potato flour (see Glossary)
60 g (2 oz) minced (ground) chicken
garlic, minced
1 chilli, chopped and deseeded
3 snow peas, cut into 2 cm (¾ in) pieces
3 button mushrooms, cut in half
1 carrot, a few slices
1 shallot (spring onion/scallion), finely chopped

Seasoning
5 tablespoons soy paste (see Glossary)
½ teaspoon sugar
ground white pepper, a pinch

sesame oil, to drizzle

Heat a wok over high heat. When it's hot, add the oil and deep-fry the tofu until crispy and golden in colour. Remove the tofu from the wok and discard the deep-frying oil.

Combine the potato flour with 1 teaspoon of water to make a paste.

Add 1 tablespoon oil to the still hot wok. Add the chicken, garlic and chilli and stir-fry for a few minutes. Stir in the snow peas and mushrooms before adding the seasoning.

Add tofu and shallots to the wok and mix well. Stir in the potato paste to thicken the sauce, then drizzle with the sesame oil and serve.

One serve

Chinese Turnip Omelette

4 eggs
2 tablespoons Chinese turnip, minced
¼ teaspoon salt
1 shallot (spring onion, scallion), finely chopped
½ teaspoon sugar
2 tablespoons vegetable oil
coriander (cilantro), to serve

Lightly beat the eggs and add all the remaining ingredients.

Heat the wok and add the oil. When it's very hot, add the egg mixture. Stir constantly until almost set then turn heat to medium. Use a spatula to shape the omelette. When golden, turn over and fry for a few minutes.

Garnish with coriander and serve.

One serve

Chinese Turnip Congee

250 g (8 oz) rice
2 tablespoons dried shrimp
3.75 litre (8 pint) water
60 ml (2 fl oz) vegetable oil
150 g (5 oz) pork, minced (ground)
50 g (2 oz) Chinese turnip, finely chopped

Seasoning
1 teaspoon salt
1 teaspoon bonito powder (see Glossary)
ground white pepper, a pinch

2 shallots (spring onions/scallions), finely chopped
1 stick celery, finely chopped

Wash rice well and drain.

Soften the shrimp in water then drain.

Bring rice and water to the boil in a large pot, stirring constantly to avoid the rice from sticking to the pot. Once the water is boiled, turn the heat down to simmer and cook the rice without a lid.

While the rice cooks, heat the wok over high heat then add the oil.

Stir-fry the pork, turnip, shrimp and seasoning until fragrant.

Once the rice is cooked, add the turnip mixture and bring back to the boil. Remove the pot from the heat.

Add the shallots and celery to the congee, mix through well and serve.

One serve

Water Spinach with XO Sauce

Tossing Sauce
1 tablespoon XO Sauce (see Glossary)
½ teaspoon salt
1 teaspoon sugar
1 small chilli, thinly sliced at an angle
2–3 cloves garlic, sliced

400 g (13 oz) water spinach, cut in 2–3 cm (¾i n) pieces
2 tablespoons XO Sauce, to serve

Combine tossing sauce ingredients in a large bowl.

Boil a pan of water to blanch the water spinach, remove from the pan once the water comes back to the boil. Drain well.

Combine the spinach with the tossing sauce and mix well. Transfer to a plate and top with the remaining XO Sauce.

Serve.

One serve

Note
XO sauce can also be purchased ready-made from Asian grocery stores.

Stir-fried Chinese Cabbage with Crispy Egg Strips

300 g (9½ oz) Chinese cabbage
80 ml (2½ fl oz) vegetable oil
1 egg
1 chilli, chopped
½ teaspoon salt
½ teaspoon sugar
½ teaspoon bonito powder (see Glossary)
1 teaspoon potato flour (see Glossary)

Cut Chinese cabbage leaves into chunks and the stems into finger-sized pieces for easy stir-frying.

Combine the potato flour with 1 teaspoon of water to make a paste.

Heat the oil in a wok over high heat. Add the egg and stir with chopsticks in a circular motion, until the egg is slightly set. Lower the heat to medium—this is very important otherwise the egg will not cook through evenly. Slowly stir-fry until it smells like baking a cake and separate into strips.

Remove the egg strips and leave the oil in the wok. Reheat until it's very hot, then stir-fry the cabbage until it reaches your desired texture. Add chilli, salt, sugar and bonito powder and mix through.

Return the egg strips to the wok for a final stir and mix in the potato paste to thicken the sauce.

One serve

Stir-fried Chinese Cabbage with Bacon

Many of people would be surprised to see bacon in a Chinese dish. Before refrigeration in China, pork was preserved in salt and air-dried and called 'La Rou'. If you can find modern La Rou that would be great otherwise, like my Mum has done for over 20 years, you can just use bacon. This is one of my all-time favourite dishes; I could eat it everyday!

300 g (9½ oz) Chinese cabbage,
100 g (5 oz) of bacon rashes
1 teaspoon potato flour (see Glossary)
2 tablespoons vegetable oil
1 long red chilli, sliced into rings
¼ teaspoon salt
½ teaspoon sugar
1 teaspoon bonito powder (see Glossary)

Cut cabbage leaves into chunks and the stems into finger-sized pieces for easy stir-frying. For easier stir-frying, wash cabbage in hot water and drain very well.

Cut bacon into pieces the same size as the cabbage stems.

Combine the potato flour with 1 teaspoon of water to make a paste.

Heat the wok, add oil, heat it through and then add the bacon. Stir-fry until crisp or until it releases a lovely smell. Scoop into a bowl.

Put the cabbage in the same wok and quickly stir-fry. Once cabbage has softened, add the bacon, bonito powder, chilli, salt and sugar for a quick stir. Mix in the potato paste to thicken the sauce.

Serve.

One serve

Tomato Omelette with Chicken

2 medium tomatoes
1 teaspoon potato flour (see Glossary)
60 ml (2 fl oz) vegetable oil
3–4 eggs
150 g (5 oz) chicken, cut into strips
1 teaspoon salt
2–3 teaspoons sugar
4 shallots (spring onions/scallions), chopped in 2–3cm (¾in) pieces

Cut across the top of the tomatoes and plunge into boiling water for a few minutes.

Remove from water, peel and cut into 2 cm (¾ in) cubes.

Combine the potato flour with 1 teaspoon of water to make a paste.

Heat half the oil in a wok over medium heat, lightly beat the eggs and pour them in.

Stir-fry eggs gently until they set into large-size chunks. Remove from wok.

Heat the rest of the oil in the wok and stir-fry the chicken until almost cooked. Stir in the tomatoes and shallots and cook for 1–2 minutes. Add the salt and sugar and return the egg for a quick stir.

Stir in the potato paste to thicken and serve.

One serve

Beef Fillet

250 g eye fillet, trimmed and cut into bite size pieces

Marinade
a pinch of salt
a pinch of sugar
1 tablespoon water
1/2 egg yolk
1 tablespoon potato flour
1 tablespoon vegetable oil

Sauce Mixture
1 tablespoon of shallots, finely chopped
1 teaspoon of ginger, finely chopped
1 teaspoon of white sugar
2 tablespoon soy paste
1 teaspoon steak sauce
1 teaspoon ground black pepper
200 ml (6.7 fl oz) vegetable oil, for frying
mixed leaf salad, to serve

Combine the eye fillet with salt, sugar, water and egg yolk, mixing well for a few minutes. Add in the potato flour and mix well before adding in the vegetable oil and mixing again.

Heat up the wok over medium heat, add the vegetable oil and when the wok is very hot, add in the eye fillet and stir fry for one minute.

Take the eye fillet out of the work and drain the oil. With the same wok, add in all the sauce mixture and stir on a high heat before returning the eye fillet back to the wok and tossing the eye fillet until it is well coated.

Served on a bed of mixed leaf salad.

One serve

Dry Toss Minced Pork Noodle with Soy Egg

Dry Toss Sauce
1 shallot, finely chopped
100 g (3.5 oz) of dry noodle
1 tablespoon soy paste
1 teaspoon garlic, fried
½ tablespoon shallot, fried
1 teaspoon of sugar
Sesame oil, drizzle

Chinese Greens
Soy egg (see page 214)
3 tablespoon mixed pork sauce (see page 214)

In a large pot, cook the noodles and then blanch the Chinese greens.

Drain the noodles well and place in a mixing bowl, add all ingredients and mix really well.

Place noodle in a bow and pour the minced pork sauce over the top.

Garnish with coriander, Chinese greens and soy egg to serve.

One serve

Fried Anchovy with Firm Tofu and Green Chillies

250 g (9 oz) dry/dehydrated anchovy
150 g (5 oz) firm tofu, cut into finger size pieces, about ½ cm (0.2 in)
  thickness
1 tablespoon soy sauce
1 teaspoon sugar
100 g (3.5 oz) green chilli, cut thinly on angle
50 g (1.8 oz) red chilli, cut thinly on angle
250 ml (8 fl oz) vegetable oil

Heat up the wok, on medium heat, fried the anchovy to golden/crispy, drain the anchovy well on paper towel

With the same wok, stir fried tofu to soft, drain the tofu.

Clean the wok, drizzle a little bit of vegetable oil, on medium heat, returned the tofu, add chilli, soy sauce, and sugar for a good stir, then return the anchovy for a further mix. Ready to serve.

One serve

Note
This dish can be serve hot, but taste just as nice in room temperature. The heat of chilli and crunchiness of the anchovy is very addictive.

Stir Fried Seasonal Vegetables

Vegetables are seasonal, the vegetable used in stir fried should be what's available and preferred. The recipe here is to show you the short cut of stir fried vegetables and principle behind it.

½ red capsicum
3 carrots, sliced
80 g (3 oz) snow peas
100 g (3.5 oz) Chinese cabbage, cut into bite size pieces
3 broccolli heads
1 small ginger knob, sliced
1 bunch shallots, stemmed
1 teaspoon salt
Sugar, a pinch
2 tablespoon vegetable oil
1 teaspoon potato flour
1 tablespoon water

In a heated wok, add vegetable oil, shallots and ginger and cook for few seconds before adding in the remaining vegetables. Sprinkle with salt and sugar and stir well.

Combine the potato flour and water to create the paste.

Once to desire texture, add the potato flour paster for a further mix. Ready to serve.

One serve

Note
Large quantity of fresh vegetables will bring down a heated wok within a second, then the stir-fried becomes stewed. So the easiest way is blanch the vegetable with the hot water from tap (not Kettle) and drain well just before stir-fried.

Minced Pork Sauce

5 kg (11 lb) minced pork
800 ml (28 fl oz) soy sauce
60 g (2 oz) sugar
15 g (0.5 oz) rock sugar
garlic, fried
red shallots, fried
Pepper, to season
500 ml (16 fl oz) vegetable oil

In a large wok, heat up, add vegetable oil, fried the minced pork to sear in the meat juice in batches. This is the critical step. The searing seals the flavour.

Put all the fried minced pork into a large pot and add all ingredients, and top up with water to just cover the meat.

Bring to boil, then simmer for 30 minutes.

One serve

Soy Egg

2 eggs, hard boiled
a dash of soy sauce
a pinch of cinnamon
minced pork sauce (see above)

Bring the eggs to room temperature before boiling. Place the eggs in a saucepan of cold water over medium heat. Bring to a gentle simmer, gently stirring the eggs in a clockwise direction. Simmer the eggs for 4–8 minutes. Once cooked, remove the egg from the pot and peel shell.

Place the egg in a pot over medium heat with a dash of soy sauce, at a ratio of water:soy sauce of 10:1. Add in a pinch of cinnamon and bring the pot to boil, then simmer for 5 minutes. Remove pot from heat and allow the egg to cool in the water for 2 hours.

Remove the egg from the pot and marinate in minced pork sauce overnight. This will help bring out the flavours in the soy egg.

Pork Belly Stir Fried with Ginger and Bamboo Shoot (Dry Menma)

150 g (5 oz) pork belly, thinly sliced to finger size
200 g (6.5 oz), reconsititue/rehydrate with water, cut to the same length and
  the pork belly
20 g (0.6 oz) ginger, shredded
2 stem shallots, cut to same length as the pork belly
Red chilli, add a few slices for flavlour
3 tablespoon soy sauce
½ teaspoon sugar
2 tablespoons vegetable oil

Heat up the wok, high heat, add oil, stir fried the pork belly to almost well done, add ginger and bamboo to further stir-fry.

Add shallot and chilli for another lightly stir. Add soy sauce and sugar, mix well to serve.

One serve

> **Note**
> With dehydrated (dry menma), it takes days to reconstitute with water, the water needs to be changed daily until the bamboo is only lightly fragrant and soft.

Pork Belly Stir Fried with Firm Tofu

150 g (5 oz) pork belly, thinly sliced to finger size
150 g (5 oz) firm tofu cut to finger size
1 red chilli, cut thinly on angle
Shallot, 3 stems, cut into 5cm strips
3 tablespoon soy sauce
½ teaspoon sugar
2 tablespoon vegetable oil

Heat up the wok, add oil, on medium heat, stir fried tofu to soft, drain the tofu

With existing oil in the wok, stir fried the pork belly to almost done, return the tofu together with chilli, shallot for further stir.

Add soy sauce and sugar, mix well, ready to serve.

One serve

Note
In the initial stage, heat control for tofu is important, do not over fried the tofu.

Desserts

Sticky Rice with Wolfberries and Sultanas Served with Sweet Peanut Powder and Coriander

500 g (16 oz) sticky rice
2 tablespoons sugar
2 tablespoons Chinese wolfberries (see Glossary)
2 tablespoons sultanas
4 tablespoons sweet peanut powder (see Glossary)
1 stalk coriander (cilantro), chopped

Soak the rice for 4 hours, then drain.

Place the rice in a steamer and poke holes through it with a chopstick to allow the steam to get through. Steam for 30 minutes.

When cooked, place in a bowl and stir in the sugar.

Mix the wolfberries and sultanas together.

Line 6 small bowls with cling film.

Place a spoon of the wolfberries and sultana mix in the bottom of each bowl and pack the rice in over the top—fill it well so it takes on the shape of the bowl.

Allow to cool to room temperature.

Invert each bowl onto a serving plate. Sprinkle the sweet peanut powder and chopped coriander around the dessert and serve.

Makes 6

Sticky Rice Cakes in Ginger Syrup with Sweet Peanut Powder

My Mum always makes a large quantity of these and freezes them so we can have them as a treat any time.

½ kg (1 lb) glutinous rice flour
400 ml (13.5 fl oz) water

500 g (16 oz) sugar
250 ml (8 fl oz) water
1 piece ginger
sweet peanut powder (see Glossary), to serve

Thinly slice the ginger and wash the slices. This preserves a good colour.

Boil the ginger, sugar and water until sugar dissolves.

Mix the flour and water together (it will be on the dry side similar to a scone mixture). Make one small patty from about one tenth of the mix and drop this into boiling water. When it floats and expands, take it out of the water and return it to the remaining flour and water mix.

Knead the patty back into the mix. The water it absorbed during cooking will be enough to moisten all the flour.

Knead well then roll and flatten into patties about 2cm–3½cm (¾–1½in) in diameter.

At this point the cakes can be frozen.

Drop them into boiling water in batches, cook for 6 minutes before removing from the water and draining.

Place the cakes on a plate, pour over the ginger syrup and add a few ginger slices. Top each rice cake with the sweet peanut powder and serve.

Makes enough for a party!

Sweet Red Bean with Vanilla Ice Cream

500 g (1 lb) red beans
375 g (13 oz) sugar or to taste
80 g (3 oz) potato flour mixed with 60 ml (2 fl oz) water to make a paste
vanilla ice cream, to serve
cocoa powder, to serve

Soak the red beans overnight to soften them.

The next day, bring them to the boil in about 2.5 litre (5 pint) of water.

Reduce the heat to very low and simmer for about 90 minutes or until the beans are soft.
Be careful not to cook them too fast or they will break apart or lose their skins.

Add the sugar to the pot and then the potato paste, which will soak up any remaining liquid and thicken the red bean.

Chill.

Serve a scoop of red bean with ice cream and dust with cocoa powder.

Serves enough for a party!

Note
Any cooked red bean that's left over can be frozen for future use. It can also be used to make red bean soup. Just add hot water and sugar to taste.

Mochi with Brown Sugar Syrup, Crushed Peanuts and Black Sesame

500 g (16 oz) glutinous flour
400 ml (13.5oz) water
2 tablespoon vegetable oil

Sugar Syrup
500 ml (16 fl oz) water
300 g (10oz) white sugar
100 g (3 oz) raw sugar
ginger, a few slices

Mix the flour and water together (it will be on the dry side similar to a scone mixture) to make the Mochi. Make one small patty from about one tenth of the mix and drop this into boiling water. When it floats and expands, take it out of the water and return it to the remaining flour and water mix.

Knead the patty back into the mix. The water it absorbed during cooking will be enough to moisten all the flour.

Once the cooked and raw dough are well mixed, add in the vegetable oil for further kneading.

Knead well then roll and flatten into patties about 5cm (2 in) in diameter. These rice cakes are commonly known as Mochi. At this point the cakes can be frozen.

Drop them into boiling water in batches, cook for 6 minutes before removing from the water and draining.

To make the sugar syrup, combine the water, white sugar, raw sugar and ginger slices in a boiling pot and leave to boil. Once the ingredients have dissolved, the sugar syrup is ready to use.

Place Mochi on a plate, drizzle over the raw sugar syrup, sprinkle with some crushed peanuts and black sesame.

Makes enough for a party

Note
Raw rice cakes can be kept in Freezer in airtight containers and any leftover sugar syrup can be refrigerated and kept for another use.

GLOSSARY OF UNUSUAL INGREDIENTS

Note: Most ingredients listed below and throughout this book should be available in Asian grocery stores.

Bai-Chao (Hundred Spices): A combination of different herbs and spices. Frequently used in marinating, preserving, grilling and deep-frying. Generally very expensive and available in Chinese herbal stores.

Bean Curd Pastry: Is generally gluten free and made from yellow beans. Look for the thinnest pastry possible to give a much nicer texture when deep-frying.

Black Vinegar: Made from rice with fermented fruits and vegetables. Suitable for soups and noodles.

Bonito Flakes: Made from smoked bonito fish. They look like wood shavings. Commonly used in Japanese cooking.

Bonito Powder: A flavour enhancer made from smoked bonito fish.

Chilli Oil: Available ready-made in most Asian grocery stores.

Chilli Bean Sauce: Made from fermented soy beans with chilli and garlic. Widely used in Asian cooking and generally very salty.

Chinese Celery: Thinner and more fragrant than Western celery, the stems are longer and hollow. It is often mistaken for coriander and perfect for soups.

Chinese Wolfberries: Are orange-red, dried sultana-shaped Chinese herbs, also known as goji berries. Available in Chinese herbal stores and some Asian grocery stores.

Dumpling Pastry Wrappers: These wrappers are round and made from plain flour. Available from the refrigerator section in most Asian grocery stores.

Five Spice Powder: Available in Chinese herbal stores and Asian grocery stores. Quality varies according to herb and spices grading.

Fried Shallots: Made from red Asian shallots which are generally small in size. An essential topping ingredient in non soy sauce based soups.

Glutinous Rice Flour: Frequently used in Asian desserts to give more texture.

Huntun (Wonton) Pastry Wrappers: These thin, square wrappers are made from plain flour. They are available from the refrigerator section in most Asian grocery stores.
Potato Flour: A much better thickening agent, which gives a clearer and glossier finish than cornflour.

Preserved Chinese Plums: Are a popular Chinese snack food and available in powder also. Salty, sour and acidic in flavour.

Rice Vinegar: It should be made in a rice wine fermentation process, but generally is made from rice.

Shaoxing Rice Wine: A type of Chinese rice wine from Shaoxing County. Made from glutinous rice and wheat.

Soy paste: Much thicker than soy sauce. Not as strong in flavour as oyster sauce. Suitable for vegetarians.

Spring Roll Pastry Wrappers: Thin, elastic-like wheat based wrappers. Small, medium and large sizes are available from the refrigerator section in most Asian grocery stores.

Sweet Peanut Powder: Ground roasted peanuts mixed with castor sugar. The ration is generally 2:1.

Sweet Potato Flour: Also known as tapioca powder. It gives a much crunchier taste when deep-fried. Preferred in Taiwanese cooking and comes in a crumbed variety.

Szechuan Peppercorns: Look similar to black peppercorns and originally from Szechuan province in China. They give a much stronger aroma and flavour.

Taiwanese BBQ Sauce: Main ingredients include soybean oil, fish, garlic, spices, shallots, sesame oil, dried shrimp and chilli. Similar to what is commonly known as satay sauce.

White Rock Sugar: Are lumps of sugar which give food a cleaner taste. There is also a yellow-coloured variety available.

XO Sauce: Originated in Hong Kong in the 1980s. Main ingredients include dried scallops, dried shrimp and salted ham.

Yellow Chives: These are part of the Chinese chive family and have a lighter flavour. Generally not widely available.

Sauces you can find in your Asian grocery store.
Clockwise from left: Taiwanese barbecue sauce, soy
sauce, soy paste, black vinegar, Taiwanese rice wine
and rice vinegar.

Index

First published in 2015 by New Holland Publishers Pty Ltd

London • Sydney • Auckland

The Chandlery Unit 009 50 Westminster Bridge Road London SE1 7QY United Kingdom
1/66 Gibbes Street Chatswood NSW 2067 Australia
5/39 Woodside Ave Northcote Auckland 0627 New Zealand

www.newhollandpublishers.com

Copyright © 2015 New Holland Publishers Pty Ltd
Copyright © 2015 in text: Muriel Chen
Copyright © 2015 in images: New Holland Publishers Pty Ltd, Qing Cong Li (p 9) and Eugene Wu – Facet
Studio Architect (p 92-93)

All rights reserved. No part of this publication may be reproduced, stored in a retrieval system or transmit-
ted, in any form or by any means, electronic, mechanical, photocopying, recording or otherwise, without
the prior written permission of the publishers and copyright holders.

A record of this book is held at the British Library and the National Library of Australia.

ISBN : 9781742577487

Managing Director: Fiona Schultz
Production Director: Olga Dementiev
Project Editor: Jessica McNamara
Designer: Lorena Susak
Photography: Joe Filshie, Sue Stubbs
Food Styling: Georgie Dolling, Carolyn Fienburg
Printer: Toppan Leefung Printing Limited

10 9 8 7 6 5 4 3 2 1

Keep up with New Holland Publishers on Facebook
www.facebook.com/NewHollandPublishers